CHRISTIANITY IS RIDICULOUS

HOW MUCH DO YOU
REALLY KNOW ABOUT CHRISTIANITY?
HERE'S A QUICK WAY TO FIND OUT!

CHRISTIANITY
IS RIDICULOUS

John Allan & Gus Eyre

PATERNOSTER
PRESS

CARLISLE, UNITED KINGDOM

First published as 'Express Checkout' in 1986
by The Paternoster Press Ltd.

This revised edition 1995 by OM Publishing

01 00 99 98 97 96 95   7 6 5 4 3 2 1

OM Publishing is an imprint of Send the Light Ltd.,
P.O. Box 300, Carlisle, Cumbria CA3 0QS, U.K.

Unless otherwise stated, Scripture quotations
in this publication are from the Holy Bible,
New International Version.

British Library Cataloguing in Publication Data

Allan, John
    Christianity is Ridiculous
    I. Title II. Eyre, Gus
    230

    ISBN 1–85078–136–2

Typeset by Photoprint, Torquay, Devon
and Printed in the U.K. by Cox and Wyman Ltd., Reading

Contents

Start here

So. . . is Christianity ridiculous?
How much do you really know about it?
Here's a quick way of finding out.

This book contains a lot of evidence—names, facts, places, arguments—documenting the case for some of the things Christians believe in. We've tried to cover all the most important questions, although obviously in such a short book things have had to be telescoped a bit, and we haven't said as much as we'd have liked to in some places. But it should be enough to help you work out whether or not the whole thing really is totally stupid . . .

Perhaps you're already a Christian, on the prowl for good arguments to use in discussions, and stunning facts to amaze and impress your friends with. Fine. Page 202 has a helpful guide which will locate the page you need in a matter of seconds.

But let's assume you're a sceptical person, uncommitted, but honest and open-minded. Where would you like to start? Have a look at the following list of statements, and place a tick beside the ones you agree with.

Now pick any of the statements by which you've placed a tick. (If you haven't ticked any, you should be reading a different book!) Turn to the page shown alongside the question in the list above. And pick your own route from there!

Have an exciting time, but remember one thing. If Jesus Christ really is the truth, as Christians claim, and is still alive, and has the right to be in charge of your life—you might just find you have to make an important personal decision before you finish.

Special advice for Christians—How you can use this book

In this book we have covered far more objections than will ever be dreamt up by most individual non-Christians. So you should be well equipped with points to raise in just about every discussion, once you have managed to find your way round this book. Any evangelist will tell vou that the problems raised by non-Christians tend to be boringly repetitive! The same few arguments come up, again and again—and always as if it's the first time anyone's ever thought of anything so clever! One essential skill you may have to learn is how to stop that 'Oh yes, I've heard it all before' expression from surfacing on your face!

But at least this habit of repetition should give you courage. If you can answer just seven or eight basic questions (probably question 2 in Section 1, questions 6 and 7 in Section 2, question 2 in Section 3, question 3 in Section 4, question 1 in Section 5, question 6 in Section 6, and question 1 in Section 7!) you'll be equipped for most of the arguments that will come your way. So it might be worth taking some time to learn and perfect answers to those particular objections.

When you come up against a different question, the first thing to do is to look for it in the list at the end of the book. It may help you if you decide which of the main Sections it would most naturally belong to, and look for it there. Most answers, you will find, are organized around three or four main points; and that should help you memorize your answer, if you want to.

What if you come up against a question which doesn't seem to feature anywhere in the book? Don't panic! You will find that behind most complicated questions lies a simple assumption or two which you *can* answer. For example, someone might want to know, 'How about that new paperback, *Jesus—Son of a Werewolf*, which claims that Jesus was invented by an eighteenth century Gothic novelist?'

Your first impulse might be to think, 'Help! I've never heard of the book!' But then you notice the assumptions which lie behind the question. Things like: 'You can't trust the Gospels as information sources'. 'You can't prove conclusively that Jesus ever existed'. 'There is no way you can be sure that Jesus is real'. And you think, 'Ah! Now those I can answer. Where's my *Christianity is Ridiculous?*'

So train yourself to spot the assumptions, and you'll survive with no trouble.

But what if you are asked a question to which you can't honestly see any kind of answer at all? This will probably never happen; but we all sometimes get into situations where our brain seizes up. Well, once again, don't panic. Do three things:

(1) Admit, 'I don't know.' That will impress the questioner with your honesty. After all, you aren't intending to pose as the Mastermind of the Year answer to everything—are you?

(2) Add, '. . . But I'll find out.' This will show that you are taking the objection seriously, not just brushing it aside; and also that you have the open-mindedness to explore a bit further. You're not afraid of facts, because your faith can stand up to scrutiny.

(3) Keep your promise, and get back to the questioner with the information you've found out (ask an older Christian if you don't know where to start looking). This will probably take your whole discussion on to a new level of seriousness, as he sees that you are treating his arguments with care and thought.

Now three final pieces of advice.

Be sensitive. Realize that sometimes people put up questions as a smokescreen—not because they really want the answers, but because they are too shy to say what is really on their mind. Perhaps they are really trying to say, 'I want to become a Christian.' Or, 'You're getting too close to my deepest feelings; please back off a bit.' Or, 'I just don't want to think about it, and I'm going to defend myself with red herring arguments until you go away.' Whatever it is—be sensitive!

Be challenging. Too many discussions between Christians and non-Christians consist simply of arguments put up by the non-Christian, shot down by the Christian, followed by another try from the non-Christian, and another reply from the Christian—and so on, back and forth, back and forth, without actually getting anywhere. Learn how to turn your answers into questions! Be able to move from defence into attack. For example, once you have answered the objection, 'How could God condemn those who have never heard?', instead of waiting expectantly in silence for his next try, you could say, 'But that's what the Bible says about those who have *never* heard. Now let me ask you a question. Where do you think that leaves *you*?' This kind of counter-challenge prevents the discussion from becoming just an abstract, impersonal argument, with no real practical application whatsoever.

Be humble. Realize that if your friend does become a Christian, it won't ultimately be your clever arguments that have persuaded him—but God's Spirit bringing him to a conviction of his need of the Lord Jesus. So relax! Just because you forget your fifth subpoint about the circumstances of the resurrection, all is not going to be lost! The responsibility ultimately rests with God and not with you.

But that does mean that you need to pray seriously about everything you do. Never assume that your ability to reason will carry you through on your own. And learn some other skills as well: how to explain the basic facts of the gospel, clearly and simply; how to give your own story about how you became a Christian, crisply, concisely, and in understandable language; and how to lead someone to Christ when he is ready to make his commitment.

If you do this basic bit of homework, I'm convinced you will find God putting you into more and more exciting adventures in communication, sharing your faith and the 'reason for the hope that is in you' with more and more people. So be prepared—and have a great time!

QUESTIONS ABOUT GOD

You have said that you agree with the statement:

I can't accept the Bible's view of God

This could be your opinion for several reasons. Here are some of the most common reasons people come up with. Tick whichever one(s) may apply to you.

☐ If God made everything, who made God? (p. 6)
☐ Our scientific understanding of the origins of
life casts doubt on the idea of God (p. 7)
☐ The idea of evolution does away with the need
for God (p. 9)
☐ There are lots of different religions which could
be just as true as Christianity (p. 10)
☐ The God of the Bible is a bloodthirsty tyrant (p. 12)
☐ The idea of 'God' is philosophically
meaningless, emotional language (p. 13)
☐ The concept of God arose from primitive
superstitions (p. 15)
☐ If God wants us to believe in him, he should
make himself visible (p. 16)
☐ If God knew we would make a mess of this
planet, it was irresponsible of him to create it (p. 18)
☐ A God who demands his son's death before his
bloodlust is appeased isn't worth believing in (p. 19)

---

*Now turn to the page(s) in this Section on which the answer
is given to the statements you have ticked.*

◀ Read them, and decide what you think of the answers
supplied. Then you can go back to the START HERE page
at the beginning of the book, and choose another direction.

▶ Or if you feel you've surveyed the evidence sufficiently already, turn straight to Section 9 (YOURSELF)—on p. 187—and follow the instructions there in order to check out your own position.

If God made everything, who made God?

It sounds logical, doesn't it? Everything was made by something else. You never get an effect without a cause. So if God made everything, he must have been made, too. Who did it?

But wait a minute. If God had to be made by somebody . . . then somebody had to create whoever created God. And somebody had to make whoever made whoever made whoever made whoever made . . . You see? There's no logical stopping point. It goes back and back, and you never get any ultimate answer.

Try it. Start asking the question: 'Who made God? And who made whoever made . . .?' You'll still be feebly repeating 'whoever made whoever made . . .' three days later when they cart you off, tired and emotional, to the mental hospital.

There has to be *somebody*, or *something*, to put the whole thing in motion. One of the leaders of my former church is a Professor of Materials Science. He explains that the Second Law of Thermodynamics insists that 'you can't get owt for nowt'. (He comes from Yorkshire.) In other words, nothing just 'happens'. It all comes from somewhere. Everything going on in the universe right now demonstrates that the universe is running down, like a clock that was once wound up. Somebody—or something—must have wound it up . . .

And scientists have begun to notice recently that the whole thing is designed with incredible exactness (more about this on pp. 9–10). It's as if we were 'written into the plans of the universe', to quote a scientist on the radio recently. Sir Bernard Lovell, the great astronomer, has asked: 'Is the universe the way it is, because it was necessary for the existence of man?'

It makes sense to me to believe that a planning intelligence created what I see around me. That when you reach the ultimate point from which everything started, you find a God, outside space and time, who has always been there (except that 'always' doesn't mean much outside space and time!) and who designed reality the way it is. It does not make sense to believe everything just happened by accident . . .

Do you find this a convincing answer?
☐ YES   ☐ NO   ☐ POSSIBLY

If you have further objections to the Bible's view of GOD, read some other parts of this section (pp. 5–21)

Alternatively you might be asking:

If the world was created by a good God, why are people fighting one another? (turn to p.143)

Our scientific understanding of the origins of life casts doubt on the idea of God

No question about it, Darwin's *Origin of Species* shattered the faith of a lot of people. Many nineteenth century Westerners who had grown up with the idea that humankind was a special creation of God, a totally unique being, suddenly found themselves confronted with evidence that all life forms had developed by change from simple and humble origins . . . and God needn't be involved at all. Charles Darwin was studying for the ministry when he went on the famous voyage of the Beagle; he wasn't when he came back.

But over the last few years a lot of (non-Christian) scientists have started to have doubts about the accuracy of Darwin's reasoning. At a conference in 1967 Professor Murray Eden of the Massachusetts Institute of Technology showed that if only six mutations were required to bring about one adaptive change in a living species, it would happen by chance only once in a billion years. And if (much more likely) two dozen genes were involved, that would take ten billion years—longer than the age of the earth!

From another scientific field, Robert Jastrow, director of NASA's Goddard Institute for Space Studies, has confirmed that 'the essential elements in the astronomical and biblical accounts of Genesis are the same: the chain of events leading to man commenced suddenly and sharply at a definite moment in time, in a flash of light and energy . . . we scientists did not expect to find evidence for an abrupt beginning'.[1] His article was headed 'Have Astronomers Found God?'

Says Gordon Rattray Taylor, 'The bland confidence . . . that all can be explained in terms of mutation and natural selection seems distinctly misplaced.'[2] There is too much evidence of purpose behind creation. At the precise moment of the 'Big Bang', two forces—gravity and the weak nuclear force—had to be tuned to each other to an accuracy of 1 in 10^{60}. Otherwise the galaxies would never have formed. And this is the accuracy a rifleman would need if he were to hit a one-inch target at the other side of the universe—twenty billion light years away. Chance?

Do you find this a 'convincing answer?
☐ YES   ☐ NO   ☐ POSSIBLY

If you have further objections to the Bible's view of GOD, read some other parts of this section   *(pp. 5–21)*

Alternatively you might be asking:

Why does God allow natural disasters like earthquakes and volcanoes?   (Turn to p.145)

The idea of evolution does away with the need for God

Now why should you think that? Probably you're making one of two wrong assumptions. You could be thinking, 'Evolution contradicts the Bible'; or you could be thinking, 'Evolution explains how everything happened without needing to drag God in'. Let's examine both ideas.

First, the Bible. You'll notice that Genesis (where the Bible's creation story occurs) is not subtitled *A Scientific Treatise: How I Made the World, By God*. It doesn't claim to be giving a scientific account—and to criticize it as science would be like criticizing the London Area telephone directory for not having much of a story line.

If Genesis had been written in scientific terminology, nobody in history until now would have been able to understand it. And—judging by the rate at which scientific knowledge is increasing—it would be out of date again twenty years from now! Instead, God has put his statement in the timeless form of a simple story anyone can understand, in any civilization—a memorable picture of a man, a woman, a garden, a snake. . .

(So does that mean evolution happened? I haven't a clue. All I'm saying is that scientists are exploring how things happened, and the Bible is telling us why—which is a different question. It does so in remarkably simple, dignified language. Who takes seriously nowadays the bloodthirsty, bizarre creation myths of the Babylonians and Assyrians? Yet these were much more sophisticated civilizations than that of the small, scruffy Near Eastern tribe who produced Genesis . . .)

Second: does evolution explain everything away? Wrong, and wrong again. It offers no explanation of where matter came from in the first place. Of what happened to cause the primordial explosion which formed the galaxies and solar systems. Of how the most complicated changes could possibly have come about by chance. (Darwin himself confessed, 'When I think of the eye, I shudder.' The delicacy and complexity involved in the human eye seemed to prove that we aren't just accidental.)

Professor H. Quaestler has calculated that the chances of the raw materials of life 'just happening' are 1 in 10^{301}. Other estimates go as high as 10^{600}. And you think evolution explains everything away? Pull the other one.

⚖️   *Do you find this a convincing answer?*
     ☐ YES   ☐ NO   ☐ POSSIBLY

❗   *If you have further objections to the Bible's view of GOD, read some other parts of this section*   *(pp. 5–21)*

❓   *Alternatively you might be asking:*

But haven't archaeological discoveries exploded many Bible claims?   (Turn to p. 59)
Isn't it arrogant to believe that human life matters in a meaningless universe?   (Turn to p.155)

There are lots of different religions which could be just as true as Christianity

'All right, I'll buy the idea of God. There has to be something out there . . . something bigger than us . . . But how can you be sure you know the truth about it? Why the Christian God, rather than any other one?'

Let me give you three reasons to think about. First, the Christian idea of God satisfies more of the real needs of human beings than any other. The great Eastern religions talk about a God who is ultimately impersonal—a force, like electricity or the wind—what C. S. Lewis called 'an infinitely extended rice pudding'. The traditional Western religions talk about gods who are human all right—the Pantheon of Greece or Rome, the Norse gods—but they're not very divine: they lie, cheat, fornicate, brawl, and fall out of heaven. Only in Christianity do you find a God who is both transcendent and personal —and who has come so close to human beings that he was actually born as a human baby.

Second, Christianity fulfils people as nothing else can. Vijay Menon was a proud Hindu, with a deep knowledge of Islam, and nothing but scorn for Christianity. But he came to see that he was missing the greatest thing in life by rejecting Christ. 'I know that Jesus is the only Way,' he says today. 'In other religions people are always seeking, always looking at what man has written about God . . . Now I love God out of thankfulness for what he has done for me.'[3]

Third, and this is the clincher, Christianity lays itself open to verification as no other religion does. The Bible insists that you can prove to yourself, in your own experience, whether Jesus' claims were true or not—by inviting him to take charge of your life and transform your experience. 'If anybody is a Christian,' claims the Bible, 'he is a brand new person inside.' If you give your life into Jesus' control, and nothing happens, you've disproved Christianity. But as millions have found, Jesus never lets people down—he keeps his promises. And the experience of Jesus' reality and friendship leaves no room for doubt. He is the Way!

⚖️ *Do you find this a convincing answer?*
☐ YES ☐ NO ☐ POSSIBLY

❗ *If you have further objections to the Bible's view of GOD, read some other parts of this section* (pp. 5–21)

❓ *Alternatively you may be asking:*

But don't all religions lead to God? (Turn to p. 73)

But isn't it arrogant to force your religion on others? (Turn to p.111)

The God of the Bible is a bloodthirsty tyrant

When you read stories in the Old Testament which talk about bears coming out of the forest and ripping apart little children who dared to call a prophet names, and battles in which God tells the Israelites not to spare any of their enemies or their children, it's easy to assume that the God of the Bible is a fairly repulsive character. And what about all the animal sacrifices? Not to mention the fact that he forced his own son to die (see p. 19 on that one) and that Christianity has been causing bloody wars ever since (see p. 81 on that).

Bloodthirsty? But when you compare the Old Testament social code and legal system with those of other nations in the same period of history, you find a tremendous difference. The Old Testament is always concerned with the right and the value of the individual—no matter how poor or vulnerable he might be. It was a humane system which took direct action against economic oppression. Unlike other nations, the Jews believed God was concerned about justice and equality, and consequently they were years ahead of their time.

What about the gory bits? Well, remember that the Bible wasn't all written in the same week! It contains the story of how God progressively revealed more and more of his character and his nature to a small tribe who were rising from primitivity to civilization. Naturally, he didn't say everything to them at once; and sometimes the rules he made for them were stop-gaps, to be improved later when their moral awareness had increased. (One day Jesus was asked about Moses' ruling on divorce, and he said, 'Moses permitted you to divorce your wives because your hearts were hard. But it was not this way from the beginning.' And then he went on to deepen and intensify the biblical teaching on divorce.) Jesus brought in a new dimension, a whole new ethical understanding; yet he insisted that he wasn't changing God's law, and that far from being bloodthirsty, it could all be summed up in two commands which were about love.

In actuality there weren't all that many people killed in Old Testament stories. In the century of Auschwitz, Kampuchea, the Gulag Archipelago, you might well ask whether our moral sense is so much more keenly developed that we can sit in judgement on them . . .

Do you find this a convincing answer?
□ YES   □ NO   □ POSSIBLY

If you have other objections to the Bible's view of GOD, read some other parts of this section   *(pp. 5–21)*

Alternatively you might be asking:

Why does God allow believers to suffer—isn't that cruel?   (Turn to p.151)
But how could a God of love let people go to hell?   (Turn to p. 127)

The idea of 'God' is philosophically meaningless, emotional language

Here's an idea that appeals to a lot of people. Perhaps the debate about whether God exists or not is a waste of time—because the whole idea of 'God' doesn't make sense anyway! If that's true, you cut through a lot of complicated arguments, and sweep the problems out of the way at a stroke. What a time-saver!

The idea comes from the eighteenth century philosophy of David Hume, but was most fully developed in the 1920s by a group of philosophers based in Vienna. They invented what they called the Verification Principle. According to this Principle, no statement was truly meaningful unless you could carry out tests to verify it. So 'grass is green' is a meaningful statement (you can test it by looking at grass to see); but 'Jesus loves me' isn't. For how on earth can you test a statement like that?

This means that any talk about 'God' is just emotional, wishful language; because God can't be tested out. Hence Christian beliefs are not statements of fact. They just reflect the concealed wishes of the person who chooses to believe them.

It sounds like a death-blow to all religion. Until you reflect that there are lots of statements the Verification Principle doesn't quite cover. 'All cyanide is deadly', for instance. You could test that assertion only by sampling every trace of cyanide in the world. But if the first bit killed you, you'd never make it through the test . . . So it's an assertion that can't be tested; yet we know it's healthy to believe that it's true!

In fact, if you apply the Verification Principle strictly, all the concepts of art, ethics, music, love and beauty have to be written off as 'meaningless'. It sounds as if you're reducing 'real life' to a pretty negligible area.

When you have disposed of God as meaningless, there's not much left of life. Michael Harrington wrote:

> After God died, Man, who was supposed to replace Him, grew sick of himself. This resulted in a crisis of belief and disbelief which made the twentieth century spiritually empty. The nineteenth century predicted often enough that the modern world would dispel faith. It did not, however, expect that it would subvert anti-faith as well.

So the Verification Principle doesn't help us much to make sense of life. And one more thing. The Verification Principle is a statement. A statement that can't be tested. So, according to itself—it must be meaningless!

⚖ *Do you find this a convincing answer?*
☐ YES   ☐ NO   ☐ POSSIBLY

❗ *If you have further objections to the Bible's view of GOD,*
read some other parts of this section   *(pp. 5–21)*

Alternatively you might be asking:

But isn't Christian experience just psychological wish fulfilment? (Turn to p. 92)
Isn't religion just a distraction when there are bigger problems to solve? (Turn to p.157)

The concept of God arose from primitive superstitions

Back at the dawn of human history, human beings lived in tribes, like the higher apes. One older male was the leader; he had all the young women of the tribe as his mates; and therefore the young men were forced out of the tribe to find a mate of their own. One day the young men decided they had had enough. They murdered their leader and father. But having done so, they were overwhelmed with guilt and needed to feel forgiveness. As a result they invented a kind of memorial ritual devoted to their father, and every year performed a ceremony of sacrifice. As the years went by, the ideas and memories connected with the father became more and more superstitious . . . until they worshipped him as a divine figure. Father had turned into—God.

That, at least, is how Sigmund Freud, founder of psychoanalysis, believed religion had come about. The main problem with his theory is that there isn't a scrap of evidence to show that any such thing ever happened. Also, this story sounds plausible in terms of Christianity and Islam—which feature heavily ideas about guilt, forgiveness and Fatherhood—but it's of no use in explaining Eastern religions, which are not so interested in those same ideas. And the whole thing depends on a comparison of human societies to ape societies—which don't in fact operate as Freud imagined! Again, Freud's ideas about the emergence of rituals and ceremonies aren't borne out by what research has been done into cultural anthropology.

Yet you still find versions of Freud's theory around today—for example, in the works of Desmond Morris, who claims that 'our immediate ancestors' invented God to 'keep the group under control' morally. But who are these 'ancestors'? If he means the Australopithecines, nothing has been found with their remains to suggest that they had any such developments. Anyway their brain size (600–700 cc) does not suggest that they'd have been able to achieve anything so complex. Once again, not a shred of proof.

What are the facts? A hundred years ago, it was assumed that religion had started with 'primitive' ideas which had gradually led on to the 'higher' belief in one God. Now we've done enough research to know that this is not the case. The earliest religious traditions we can trace, in all sorts of societies, are traditions of one, almighty, caring, Father God.

Our idea of God was there in the beginning. It was only later on that people started to get it twisted.

Do you find this a convincing answer?
☐ YES   ☐ NO   ☐ POSSIBLY

If you have other objections to the Bible's view of GOD, read some other parts of this section   *(pp. 5–21)*

Alternatively you might be asking:

But surely people are no longer religious nowadays?
(Turn to p. 101)
Isn't Christianity just pie in the sky when you die?
(Turn to p. 149)

If God wants us to believe in him, he should make himself visible

But do you believe only in what you can see? Obviously not. The reason you don't walk out of a fifth-floor window is that you believe in gravity—which you have never seen. The reason you don't thrust your fingers into a power socket is that you believe in electricity—which you have never seen. You don't *see* these things, but you *feel their effect* in your life. Maybe it could be the same way with God too? That while he stayed invisible he could nonetheless affect your circumstances so unmistakeably that it made sense to believe in him?

'Well, maybe,' you might say. 'But why *doesn't* he come out of hiding from time to time? Surely everyone would believe if they could just see him.' Really? If God appeared in front of you, he'd either look like everybody else you'd ever seen—in which case you'd have a hard time believing he was special—or else he'd appear in all his power and glory, which would blow your mind so comprehensively that you wouldn't be sure if it was a trick, or if you were hallucinating, or if you'd gone mad, or . . . The experience would be so unlike everything else that normally happened to you, that you'd find it hard to believe. At the time it might be convincing. Half an hour later you'd start thinking, 'Did that really happen or did I just imagine it?'

The reason God does not manifest himself visibly more often is that he has come as close to us already as he possibly can. When Jesus Christ was here on earth, human beings saw God. Jesus was the perfect representation of what God was like (Hebrews 1:3). And the response of evil human beings was to nail him to a cross. Would we treat him any better today?

But the cross wasn't the end. Jesus rose again and now offers a new life of freedom from evil to anyone who will believe in him and accept him as King. 'We have not seen him,' said the early Christians,'but we love him' (see 1 Peter 1:8). And one day, the Bible promises, Christians will see Jesus for themselves. So God isn't playing hide and seek behind the clouds, keeping us guessing. He is available and can be real to anyone prepared to make contact with him through Jesus.

Do you find this a convincing answer?
☐ YES   ☐ NO   ☐ POSSIBLY

If you have other objections to the Bible's view of GOD, read some other parts of this section   *(pp. 5–21)*

?

Alternatively you might be asking:

But surely Jesus himself never claimed to be God?
                                              (Turn to p. 35)
Can you be sure you know God, or is it all just wishful
thinking?   (Turn to p. 96)

If God knew we would make a mess of this planet, it was irresponsible of him to create it

God can see the future, can't he? So he must have known about Vietnam before he created the universe. And Belsen. And Stalin. And starvation in the Horn of Africa. So why did he go on to create something as terrible as this?

The trouble with this argument is that it rests on three shaky assumptions. The first is: *that God was there before the universe was*. Well, in a sense he was. But he's right outside space and time—so he's simultaneously before, after and in the middle of history! Every moment of the world's existence is just as present to him as every other—so 1859 wasn't 'last century' as far as God is concerned, and 2078 isn't in the future. It's impossible for us to imagine ourselves in the position of a being like that, and to decide how he ought to make his decisions. We simply don't have the equipment.

Second, is it true *that God could have created a better world?* Again, we can't judge; we've never seen any other worlds to compare this one with! The greatest and most dangerous gift God gave us was freedom of choice; he didn't make us mindless robots (more about this on pp. 116–118). And that means running the risk that we would misuse our freedom, and rebel against him. Which in fact is what we have done. But God can't respond simply by taking our freedom away—that would turn us into clockwork machines, programmed to follow his instructions, and the whole quality of human life would be drastically reduced.

Third, is it true *that this world is nothing but evil?* Of course it isn't. Most of us feel that life is worth living, on the whole; that's why we haven't committed suicide yet! Our experience is a mixture of good things and bad things, and nobody who has felt the thrill of falling in love, or has been swept away by the emotional power of a great piece of music, or has known moments of unexpected, absolute, sudden happiness, will really feel, 'God should never have bothered. Life is just a disaster.' Outweighing all the evil, says the Bible (Romans 8:18), is the tremendous beauty which will be the future of this planet of ours when God is fully in charge once more. VVhat we see then will make all the misery and pain of human history shrink into perspective. God's act of creation was no mistake.

⚖	*Do you find this a convincing answer?* ☐ YES ☐ NO ☐ POSSIBLY

❗	*If you have other objections to the Bible's view of GOD, read some other parts of this section* *(pp. 5–21)*

❓	*Alternatively you might be asking:*

If the world was created by a good God, where did evil come from?   (Turn to p.147)
Why hasn't Christianity brought peace to the world?   (Turn to p.153)

A God who demands his son's death before his bloodlust is appeased isn't worth believing in

Christians say that Jesus' death on the cross was a sacrifice. That he gave his life in our place, to pay the price of forgiveness for us. As a result God's wrath need not terrify us any longer; Jesus offers us a chance to 'flee from the wrath to come'. And some people are shocked.

'What a barbaric religion!' they say. 'An angry god, blood sacrifices, and demands that something has to die before wrong can be forgiven! It's horrible!'

Well, it would be if God's anger was like our anger. When we get angry, it's usually unreasonable, petulant, self-indulgent. It's because we're frustrated about something or lose self-control. But God is not like that. He is only angry *when there is a just cause*—and frankly, I'd be worried if he wasn't. I don't want a God who can look at murder, rape and genocide with a happy smile on his features. I can respect a God who hates evil.

And if God hates evil, I know when I'm honest with myself that there are a lot of imperfections inside me which he must hate too. Not that he hates me—the Bible makes it clear that he loves me (John 3:16)—but that he is angry about, and cannot turn a blind eye to, the way in which his creation has been defaced and damaged by sin.

If I am responsible for some of this sin, I am staring God's wrath in the face. But he doesn't want to punish me. And so Jesus took my place and died on the cross instead of me. Sin had to be dealt with; the price had to be paid. God couldn't just bend the rules and say, 'We'll forget about it this time, shall we?'—that would have been trivializing the problem and pretending it didn't matter. God's perfect justice demanded that the price should be paid.

But why Jesus? If he were just an innocent bystander, seized and killed as a sacrifice more or less at random, that would indeed be monstrously unfair. But *Jesus was God himself* (see p. 35), and when he died *God himself* paid the price of our freedom. It wasn't a case of God capriciously and cruelly demanding a blood offering before he would let us off the hook; rather, God met the demands of justice for us in his own person, through Jesus, at awesome cost. Barbaric? No. Wonderful.

Do you find this a convincing answer?
☐ YES   ☐ NO   ☐ POSSIBLY

!

> *If you have other objections to the Bible's view of GOD, read*
> *some other parts of this section (pp. 5–21). If you have read*
> *this whole section, go back to the START HERE page (p. 1)*
> *and choose another direction.*

?

Alternatively you might be asking:

Was Jesus really God, or was he just deranged?
(Turn to p. 42)
Surely we don't need God in order to live a good life?
(Turn to p. 167)

1. Robert Jastrow, 'Have Astronomers Found God?', *New York Times* 25 June 1978.
2. Gordon Rattray Taylor, *The Great Evolution Mystery* (London, 1984), 138.
3. Interviewed by *Decision* magazine.

QUESTIONS ABOUT JESUS

You have said that you agree with the statement

I don't believe what Christians claim about Jesus

This could be your opinion for several reasons. Here are some of the most common reasons people come up with. Tick whichever one(s) may apply to you.

☐ There is no evidence to prove that Jesus really
existed   (p. 23)
☐ The Gospels are biased propaganda
documents, not to be trusted as information
sources   (p. 25)
☐ It is incredible that Jesus never did anything
wrong   (p. 27)
☐ You can't believe in the miracles of Jesus today (p. 29)
☐ The story of the virgin birth is just a legend   (p. 31)
☐ There is no evidence that Jesus rose from the
dead   (p. 33)
☐ Jesus himself never claimed to be God   (p. 35)
☐ Jesus' basic message was just 'Love one
another', nothing more   (p. 38)
☐ Jesus and his earliest followers may have been
clever frauds   (p. 40)
☐ Perhaps Jesus was a lunatic   (p. 42)

Now turn to the page(s) in this Section on which the answer is given to the statements you have ticked.

◀ After reading them, and deciding what you think of the answers supplied, go back to the START HERE page at the beginning of the book, and choose another direction.

▶ Or if you feel you've surveyed the evidence sufficiently already, turn straight to Section 9 (YOURSELF)—on p. 187—and follow the instructions there in order to check out your own position.

There is no evidence to prove that Jesus really existed

Wouldn't it be amazing? If this Jesus—the figure countless millions have worshipped for two thousand years, the hero lovingly portrayed in pictures and paintings by generations of skilled artists—never existed at all? If a quarter of the human race were followers of a fantasy figure?

Well, could it be true? Many daring thinkers have made the suggestion. One of them was Karl Marx, and his idea that Jesus was mythical has been adopted by many Communist thinkers ever since. (However, it's worth pointing out that the USSR's own Institute of Militant Atheism now concedes that Jesus was real—after a forty-year attempt to prove he wasn't!) More recently, professor John Allegro has suggested that the name 'Jesus' was just a code-word for the sacred mushroom cult which lay behind Christianity, and Professor G. A. Wells has claimed that Paul's writings show so little interest in the historical details of Jesus' life that it is likely Jesus was a fictional figure.

But Allegro's ideas were immediately laughed out of court by other scholars, in letters to *The Times*, in scathing reviews, and in full-length studies which pointed out how embarrassingly wrong his assumptions were. And it isn't true, as Wells claims, that Paul has no interest in what Jesus was really like; actually his letters contain enough data to allow you to reconstruct a pretty thorough life of Jesus—that he was a real human being, born a Jew descended from David, who primarily worked among Jews, set an example of self-sacrifice and courage under persecution, instituted the Lord's Supper just before he died, was arrested by treachery, died on a cross, rose from the dead after three days and appeared to over 500 people!

Actually very few people today would seriously claim that Jesus never existed. There is just too much evidence that he did. He is mentioned, for example, by all sorts of non-Christian writers—the great Jewish historian Josephus and the great Roman historian Tacitus; other Roman writers such as Pliny, Suetonius, Lucian; traditions left by Jewish rabbis in the *Mishna* and the *Gemara*.

Inscriptions have been found on walls in such places as Pompeii (destroyed by a volcano in AD 79, just a few decades after Jesus' death) which show quite clearly that the stories about Jesus were already known and believed there.

And consider this. Something pretty big had to happen to explain the impact Christianity made in its earliest days. We know that just a few weeks after this 'mythical' hero's death there were over five thousand people in the city where he had died who already believed in his claims. Now could you really invent an imaginary person, set his adventures in your own locality, and then expect sane local people (who well knew the story was a fabrication) to start joining your organization in large numbers?

Do you find this a convincing answer?
☐ YES   ☐ NO   ☐ POSSIBLY

If you have further objections to Christian claims about JESUS, read some other parts of this section   (pp. 22–44)

Alternatively you might be asking:

If Jesus existed, did he intend to start an organization?
(Turn to p. 78)
Surely we can't trust what the Bible says anyway, because it's full of errors?   (Turn to p. 48)

The Gospels are biased propaganda documents, not to be trusted as information sources

While it's true that Jesus is mentioned by quite a few non-Christian authors of the same period, it has to be admitted that most of what we know about him comes from Matthew, Mark, Luke and John. But can they be trusted?

Obviously, they weren't objective academic historians. They were writing in order to try to convince people. John admitted, 'Jesus did many other miraculous signs . . . But these are written that you may believe that Jesus is the Christ, the Son of God . . .'[1] So they had an axe to grind. And it's obvious that they weren't interested in putting things down in chronological order; the different Gospels change the order of events of the same stories. Sometimes they seem to differ about who actually said what (although never where anything important is concerned). Clearly, they weren't historians of a modern kind.

All this led one great biblical scholar earlier this century—Rudolf Bultmann—to assert, 'I do indeed think that we can now know almost nothing concerning the life and personality of Jesus, since the early Christian sources show no interest in either, are moreover fragmentary and often legendary.'[2] Is that really the position?

Many scholars now think that Bultmann despaired too soon. For one thing, the Gospels have been shown again and again to have a strict regard for historical accuracy. (Seventy years ago, university lecturers used to compare Luke to the Greek writer Herodotus, to show how good a historian Herodotus was and how defective Luke was; as a result of our discoveries since then, they now talk about how unreliable Herodotus is, and how scrupulous Luke is!) Archaeological discoveries have backed up details in the Gospels over and over again.

Also, we now know that the Gospels come from a very early date. The first of them was written between twelve and thirty years after the events it describes—and it was circulated among Jesus' enemies, as well as his friends. If it had contained untrue claims and misleading information about Jesus, it would never had stood a chance of being believed. It had to be accurate in order to win a hearing.

There were lots of attempts to change the Gospels. Some people wanted to cut bits out, others to mnelt them down into one book, others to add fanciful stories about extra miracles and wonders. But, as Professor Xavier Leon-Dufour has clearly shown, the early church resisted all these attempts. The Christians were determined to hang on to these four vital accounts and not to change a word—because they represented the genuine facts about Jesus.

And when you look at what the Gospels have to say, it is obvious that the picture of Jesus they present is incredibly convincing and real. Jean Jacques Rousseau himself admitted, 'The Gospel has marks of truth so great, so striking, so perfectly inimitable, that the inventor of it would be more astonishing than the hero.' And Malcolm Muggeridge agreed, 'The story is so incredibly vivid that I swear to you that no one who has ever tried to write can doubt its authenticity.'[3]

Were the Gospel writers the most skilful novelists in history? Or were they simply reporting the truth?

⚖️ *Do you find this a convincing answer?*
☐ YES   ☐ NO   ☐ POSSIBLY

❗ *If you have further objections to Christian claims about JESUS, read some other parts of this section* (pp. 22–44)

❓ *Alternatively you might be asking:*

How do we know the right books are in the Bible, since some others were suppressed?   (Turn to p. 46)
Aren't there so many differences between the various manuscripts that you can't be sure what the Bible originally said?   (Turn to p. 50)

It is incredible that Jesus never did anything wrong

Personally I wouldn't fancy standing up in front of a hostile crowd challenging them: 'Can any of you prove me guilty of sin?' I don't think any of us would. As soon as we made our claim to be perfect, someone would thumb through his diary and come up with the facts and dates to prove conclusively that we'd blotted our copybook more than once . . .

Yet, if John 8:46 is to be believed, Jesus Christ was able to do just this. And no-one could successfully contest his claim. To us, living in an age of sleaze, tabloid scandals and damaging revelations about the life of the great, this may well seem incredible. Jesus never did anything wrong? What sort of Sunday school fantasy is this?

The interesting thing is that people seem to have made this claim, and believed it, right from the start. The Gospels were written soon after Jesus' death (see p. 25), when it would have been easy for hostile Jews with long memories to produce shattering contrary evidence. Yet they didn't. You find a few allegations against Jesus in writings of the time—that he was the son of an adulteress, that he did his miracles by sorcery—but not one single specific claim of anything he ever did that was wrong. The silence is impressive.

And Christians never doubted it. Around the fringes of the church there were always heretics who questioned most things the church believed about Jesus—but this idea was never contested.

Says the *Evangelical Dictionary of Theology*, 'This has been a universal conviction of the Christian church. Even heretics in the early centuries and during the later period of rationalism . . . left this teaching alone.'[4]

If we find it hard to imagine someone absolutely perfect, we need to remember that this doesn't mean that Jesus was a smug little monster who never had to go through the same stages of growing up and learning as other children.

'As Jesus grew up he advanced in wisdom and in favour with God and man.' In other words he progressed from

ignorance to knowledge. He had to learn Aramaic and
presumably made the same sort of mistakes in his tenses as
children do today . . . In the same way he learned about his
environment . . .

None of this affects the claim to sinlessness. To be less
than complete is not to be inferior . . . Growth in any area
depends on things happening to you and on your respond-
ing to them.[5]

Sometimes people object that there are two incidents in the
Gospels that show Jesus as imperfect: the cleansing of the
temple (John 2:13–16) and the cursing of the fig tree (Mark
11:12–21). They claim that Jesus here loses his temper in a very
embarrassing way. But this is silly. If Jesus really had been
losing his temper, would the evangelists (who believed Jesus
was perfect) have put the story in their Gospel—without any
explanation or attempt to justify it?

In fact, in the first case he was genuinely angry but self-
controlled; feeling angry is not a sin—losing your temper is. In
the second case, he was using the fig tree to teach his disciples
an important lesson (Mark 11:22–26).

It isn't difficult to find imperfections in the story of Karl
Marx, the Buddha, Mohammed, Confucius. With Jesus Christ,
it's remarkably difficult. Is it possible that he really was
perfect?

Do you find this a convincing answer?
☐ YES   ☐ NO   ☐ POSSIBLY

*If you have further objections to Christian claims about
JESUS, read some other parts of this section   (pp. 22–44)*

Alternatively you might be asking:

But surely you can't take the Bible literally today?
(Turn to p. 61)
Perhaps Jesus was perfect, but surely Christians are no
better than other people?   (Turn to p. 95)

You can't believe in the miracles of Jesus today

When I was studying English at university I had to translate the Old English text *The Life of St. Edmund*. It's full of stories about miracles performed by the saint, and even by his holy bones after his death. The tone of it is hectic, excited and awestruck. I didn't believe a word of it; it was just piling wonders on top of each other, quite uncritically.

Now there are books about Jesus which do the same thing. They are known as the Apocryphal Gospels; they were produced a century or two after Jesus' own day by imaginative embroiderers who knew nothing of' the real facts. The church never accepted them for a moment. Jerome wrote derisively of the *'deliramenta apocryphorum'*, 'the ravings of the Apocryphals'). As far as the church was concerned, there were only four sober, trustworthy accounts of Jesus' life, and they clung to these four obstinately. These Gospels went back almost to the day of Jesus himself (see p. 25) and told the truth.

And it's interesting, when you read the four Gospels, to see how unexcited they are about the miracles. Sure, they happened. But the Gospel writers take them in their stride, and make nothing much of them. They are not interested in recounting wonder stories; John even ends his Gospel by saying dismissively, 'Jesus did many other things as well. If every one of them were written down, I suppose that even the whole world would not have room for the books that would be written.'[6]

Jesus himself made it clear that miracles *by themselves* proved nothing. He forecast that people would come after him who would be able to do signs and wonders (Mt. 24:24) but would not be speaking the truth. His miracles weren't Superman-style feats intended to stun the credulous public; they were just visual aids, 'signs' which pointed to what his mission was all about.

The miracles were written about in the very earliest accounts of Jesus, not long after his death, when enemies could easily have denied any story which wasn't exactly true. But in fact

you don't find contemporary writers claiming that the miracles
never happened! Some Jewish opponents tried to explain
them away as magic and sorcery. A Samaritan historian
claimed that the darkness which covered the land at the
crucifixion was actually a solar eclipse. *But no-one denied the
miraculous events had taken place.* It isn't until two hundred years
later that you first find someone advancing the theory,
'Perhaps they were just legends.' People at the time knew
better.

It has been suggested that the miracles weren't actually
supernatural, but just employed physical principles which
science has not yet discovered. Well, possibly. But how come a
Galilean carpenter knew more about applied science than the
greatest minds of our century?

Dale Rhoton sums up the position like this.

> The basic issue at stake is whether one will accept the
> supernatural at all. If there really is a God, then it logically
> follows that he may suspend any law of nature if he so
> desires. And if Jesus was truly God, this power must have
> extended to him also.[7]

Do you find this a convincing answer?
☐ YES   ☐ NO   ☐ POSSIBLY

*If you have further objections to Christian claims about
JESUS, read some other parts of this section   (pp. 22–44)*

Alternatively you might be asking:

Can't the Bible be read in many different ways—so that
any interpretation could be correct?   (Turn to p. 53)
How come God doesn't do miracles today?
                                        (Turn to p. 178)

The story of the virgin birth is just a legend

There is nothing that rouses more scepticism in a twentieth century audience than a story about sex. We've grown used to scandalous revelations and Sunday newspaper exposés which reveal that many seemingly virtuous people lead lives which aren't exactly as pure as the driven snow. And so, when it confronts the story of a virginal girl having a baby, our century immediately responds by laughing in disbelief. We know it doesn't happen. However Jesus was born, it couldn't have been that way.

It doesn't help us to believe when some church leaders refer to 'the symbolic and mythological nature of the story of the virgin birth'. It sounds like a polite, scholarly way of saying, 'It's not true.' And when we find that only two of the four Gospels actually mention the claim—and it isn't mentioned anywhere else in the New Testament—and Jesus is referred to in two Gospels as 'the son of Joseph'—and there are lots of pagan myths about gods having intercourse with human females—we can easily assume it's an open and shut case. The virgin birth never happened.

But wait a minute. We do know that Christians believed in it right from the earliest days—writers like Ignatius (who died as early as 107 AD), Aristides, Justin Martyr and Tatian all held to it. No-one in the early church dissented from it (except groups of heretics, the Ebionites and Gnostics, whom you couldn't seriously call Christians anyway). If the New Testament rarely mentions it, that's not because nobody believed it—but because it was so well accepted that no-one thought it worth mentioning. Paul never built any of his doctrinal arguments around it. And if the story wasn't at all important in order to prove Christian arguments or back up Christian doctrines, why on earth would the Gospels invent a story as outlandish as that?

People in those days knew the facts of life as well as us. They didn't assume babies came from behind gooseberry bushes. And the writer of one of the Gospels which mention the virgin birth—Luke—was actually a doctor, as well as a historian so careful that Sir William Ramsay concluded after a lifetime's study, 'This author should be placed along with the very greatest of historians.' He was not likely to fabricate fairy tales which would just have got his book laughed out of court by anybody with half a brain.

Why is Jesus called 'the son of Joseph'? Because once Joseph had married his mother, in the eyes of the law, he became father to Jesus. Which is why the ancestry of Jesus in both Matthew and Luke is traced through Joseph. It would be incredibly careless for Matthew and Luke to invent a story about Jesus' miraculous birth, and then forget all about it and start contradicting themselves.

Incidentally, close analysis shows that both Gospels drew their story from different, independent sources. They weren't cooking up something between themselves but reporting the memories of two distinct groups of observers.

What about all those Greek myths? There are plenty of stories of gods coming to earth and having sexual experiences with women—but not one of a virgin birth. The Gospels do not draw anything from those pagan stories (they seem uninterested in the sexual element) but instead say something quite new and unparalleled.

If you had wanted people to believe in your leader, you wouldn't have invented such a bizarre story as that. If your leader had been born illegitimate you'd have tried to hush it up, not draw attention to it by such a ridiculous claim. You would not have insulted the intelligence of Gentiles, nor outraged the Jews by importing oriental myths into their proud national faith. That way, you'd never had made a single convert.

Unless, of course, it was true.

Do you find this a convincing answer?
☐ YES   ☐ NO   ☐ POSSIBLY

If you have further objections to Christian claims about JESUS, read some other parts of this section (pp. 22—44)

Alternatively you might be asking:

But why the Bible anyway? Aren't other sacred books
just as valuable? (Turn to p. 57)
But does it matter what you believe, as long as you're
sincere? (Turn to p. 113)

There is no evidence that Jesus rose from the dead

Now that's a brave statement to make. Because the evidence
for the resurrection is actually one of the strongest cards in
Christianity's pack. Hundreds of investigators have set out to
debunk the resurrection claim—and have ended by becoming
convinced that it actually happened. In any good bookshop
you'll find a copy of Frank Morison's *Who Moved the Stone?*, a
classic written in 1930 by a young lawyer and journalist who
felt sure he could explain away the Bible story. The second
chapter is called 'The book that refused to be written'. Guess
what happened to Frank Morison?

More recently, *The Easter Enigma* was written by a biblical
scholar who had lived in Jerusalem for several years, and so
knew the exact layout of the physical location in which all the
events took place. He was sure, before he began, that there
was no way in which the varying accounts in the different
Gospels could be made to agree with one another. To his
surprise, there was. They were telling one consistent story. It
all had the ring of truth.

And that's why the resurrection has been called—with only
a little exaggeration—'the best attested fact in ancient history'.
Because we know so much of the circumstances surrounding
the death and resurrection of Jesus Christ, that if the idea of
someone rising from the dead wasn't so bizarre, every
historian in the world would accept it as probable.

Why is this? We have no space here to examine all the
evidence. You could read Michael Green's *The Day Death Died*
(Hodder) or J. N. D. Anderson's *Christianity: The Witness of*

History (IVP) should you wish to look at it in detail. Let me just make four points to get you started.

First, Jesus really died. There was a claim, first made in the eighteenth century, that Jesus had simply fainted on the cross, then revived in the cool air of the tomb. This is impossible. First, even if there were a flicker of life left in him, the cold of a rock tomb would immediately have induced a catatonic seizure and brought death. Second, with his hands and feet shattered by nails he was in no condition to climb out of his bindings, push away a heavy stone, and escape down the road into the city—then convince his followers he had risen again in power and strength! He'd have been a pretty pathetic sight.

When Jesus' body was taken down from the cross it was examined (twice) by a Roman officer who must have seen literally hundreds of Jews die by crucifixion. He would not have let such a controversial corpse out of his safe keeping without being sure the man was dead.

Second, we know Jesus' body disappeared. There was a real mystery about it. When the disciples began proclaiming that Jesus had risen and the tomb was empty, the authorities tried to hush them up, but were unable to produce the body to show the claim was untrue. It was thoroughly embarrassing, but they just didn't know where the body had gone! And so thousands of people became Christians in the very city where Jesus had died, just six weeks after his burial.

Third, there was no way for anyone to steal the body. The grave was guarded by a body of soldiers—most likely a Roman century, which would mean up to thirty men on duty at once for a three-hour period of watch. It isn't likely that they would all fall asleep simultaneously and so allow the disciples to steal the body! If they did, the disciples couldn't have got it away into the city again—the road was lined with houses; and at this hot time of year people slept outside by the roadside. In any case, this was the one weekend in the year when no Jew was allowed to touch a dead body. A bunch of Jews carrying a corpse in the middle of the night would have been spotted by someone. And remembered.

Fourth, if the disciples stole the body, what explains their sudden change of character? From being timid, fearful and panicky, they suddenly became fearless proclaimers of the resurrection story—all over the world. They gave their lives declaring it was true. But why, if it was a hoax they had organized? It seems a bit far to take a practical joke . . .

Their behaviour makes sense only if you accept one hypothesis. That their story was actually true.

⚖️ *Do you find this a convincing answer?*
　□ YES　　□ NO　　□ POSSIBLY

❗ *If you have further objections to Christian claims about JESUS, read some other parts of this section　(pp. 22–44)*

❓ *Alternatively you might be asking:*

But surely, when you're dead, you rot?
(Turn to p. 118)
We come back for life after life anyway—don't we?
(Turn to p. 124)

Jesus himself never claimed to be God

Cirencester, in Gloucestershire, was once an old Roman garrison town called Corinium. Last century, some workmen were knocking down a wall there when they came across a strange inscription, which was obviously very old—dating from just a few years after the time of Christ. It consisted of some letters arranged in the form of a word-square, which didn't seem to mean anything very important. It spelled out a message about a sower arranging some wheels. Scholars were later mystified to find the same word square on walls in Pompeii, North Africa, and a Roman ruin near Manchester. What did it mean?

In 1926 the code was cracked. It was found that the letters could be rearranged into a cross shape, and in that form would spell out 'OUR FATHER' in Latin, in both directions. The remaining letters were 'A' and 'O'—alpha and omega, the first and last letters of the Greek alphabet—and there's a verse in the Bible acclaiming Jesus as the 'Alpha and Omega, the Beginning and the End'.

```
                                    A
  SATOR                             P
                                    A
  AREPO                             T
                                    E
  TENET                             R
                      A   PATERNOSTER      O
  OPERA                             O
                                    S
  ROTAS                             T
                                    E
                                    R
                                    O
```

The Word Square   *The Solution*

Obviously, the whole thing was one of the earliest Christian symbols—carved only a short while after Jesus' death—and it proclaimed the message that the man who had died on the cross was 'the Beginning and the End', equal in status to God, 'Our Father'. Jesus was God.

But did Jesus claim that for himself? Or was it a legend which gradually grew about him? Many people think of Jesus as just a kind prophet who was wildly misrepresented and built into a super-hero after his death. Is it true?

Well, first, as we've just seen, the belief that Jesus was God began very early in the Christian church. You can never find a stage—no matter how far back you look—when people revered Jesus as a leader, but nothing more. If he really did not make this claim, his teaching must have been distorted remarkably quickly. Some people blame the Apostle Paul for embroidering the story, and turning a Jewish rabbi into a mythological figure. But Paul's ideas about Jesus simply reflected what everyone else in the church believed a long time before he came along (see 1 Corinthians 15:3, written just thirty years after Jesus' death, when plenty of people could have denied his claim); and although he had plenty of disputes with other church leaders, no-one ever quibbled about his views on Jesus. Right from the start, the early church agreed: Jesus was God.

Did Jesus ever make the claim himself? He implied it more often than he stated it directly. His aim was to get people thinking, 'Who is he, really?' until they had worked it out for themselves. He claimed to have a relationship with God which no-one else enjoyed in the same way; he claimed to be the fulfilment of all prophecy; he claimed authority to judge all men. And every so often you do find a direct statement. Once, for example, he stated 'Before Abraham was, I AM.' This wasn't just bad grammar. 'I Am' was the sacred, unspeakable name of God—so holy that you weren't even allowed to *say* it—and here was Jesus, not only saying it, but applying it to himself. His hearers got the message all right. Immediately, we read, they started to pick up stones to throw at him. This was blasphemy . . .

How could Jesus be both 'God' and 'Son of God'? It doesn't make sense to many people. But what we need to remember is that a word like 'son', when applied to God, is picture language. You can't press the picture too far. (It doesn't, for example, mean that there has to be a 'mother' God somewhere, or that Jesus was born in some celestial maternity hospital.) The phrase 'Son of God' simply tells us how Jesus related to God the Father—with the obedience and family spirit of a perfect son—but it doesn't diminish his status. In Jesus Christ, God came to earth in human form.

Sometimes it is objected that there were other people alive in Jesus' day (such as Apollonius of Tyana) whose followers tbough they were 'sons of God'. Well, first, these other 'divine men' seem to have come after Jesus, not before—so that their followers were probably simply copying the claim the Christians were already making! And, secondly, even if claims of being a 'son of God' might have impressed Greeks and Romans, remember that the Christian church began among Jews. Every Jew was taught from his mother's knee that there was only one God, with no rivals. For people to say, 'Yes—but there's also his son . . .' would not be the best way to start a recruiting drive for a new religion! Christians would never

have invented such a controversial story unless they believed
it. Jesus was God!

| ⚖️ | *Do you find this a convincing answer?*
☐ YES   ☐ NO   ☐ POSSIBLY |

| ! | *If you have further objections to Christian claims about
JESUS, read some other parts of this section*   (pp. 22–44) |

| ? | *Alternatively you might be asking:* |

How can Jesus have been God, when his followers
have been starting wars for centuries?
(Turn to p. 81)
Isn't the idea of 'God' just emotional, philosophically
meaningless language anyway?   (Turn to p. 13)

Jesus' basic message was just 'Love one another'—nothing more

At the beginning of this century, one influential German
critic—Adolf von Harnack—insisted that the basic message of
Jesus could be boiled down to just three statements: God is our
Father; all men are brothers; individuals matter. Is this true?

Well, if Jesus had no more to say than that, it's hard to work
out why he made such an impact. As William Temple
remarked, 'Why anyone should have troubled to crucify the
Christ of Liberal Protestantism has always been a mystery.' He
would have been an inoffensive threat to nobody. And a
nonentity, too; 'Love one another' wasn't exactly a new idea,
even when Jesus came up with it. There has to be more to
explain the colossal impact of Jesus' teaching.

And when you look at what Jesus is on record as having
said, four things stand out remarkably clearly. First, *he made*

great claims for himself. He assumed he was capable of passing final judgement on other human beings. He spoke about his relationship with God the Father in terms that made it quite clear he didn't consider anybody else to be as close to God as he was. He claimed to be the fulfilment of the Old Testament, and turned upside down some of the traditional interpretations of it. Why was this simple prophet of love so bigheaded? It doesn't fit.

Second, *he claimed love was impossible without his help.* 'Separated from me,' he announced crushingly,'you can do nothing.' It wasn't just a matter of everybody pulling together to build a better world; he had to be the centre of a man's life before the man's efforts would get him anywhere. The pictures he painted of his own importance make this very clear. He was the Vine, and other humans were the branches—dead and useless unless supplied with life by the vine. He was the Light of the World, and men were lost in darkness without him. He was the Bread of Life, and without feeding on him people had no life in themselves.

Third, *he predicted that his teaching would bring hatred as well as love.* 'I did not come to bring peace,' he remarked, 'but a sword. For I have come to turn a man against his father, a daughter against her mother, a daughter-in-law against her mother-in-law . . .'[8] If people tried to follow him, they would find themselves misunderstood and sometimes persecuted by others. He was under no illusions that he could get the whole world happily loving each other. He knew that real love begins only when a person has a radical inner change, and that many people would not want him to work this change in their selfish nature.

Finally, *he talked of a final judgement,* in which there would be two sides. And the decisive issue in the judgement would be what people had done with the message Jesus came to deliver. Those who turned their back on him and rejected him would find themselves rejected by God. Jesus' message wasn't an emotional plea to the better nature of his contemporaries, to pull themselves together and spread a little sunshine around; it was an urgent warning to people of all ages, delivered with the full force and authority of God himself.

Putting it all together, Jesus sounds less and less like an amiable hippy guru of love. What his message was, you'll find spelled out more clearly on pp. 20 and 153. 'Love' had a lot to do with it, as you'll see. But that wasn't all . . .

⚖️ *Do you find this a convincing answer?*
    ☐   YES   ☐   NO   ☐   POSSIBLY

❗ *If you have further objections to Christian claims about JESUS, read some other parts of this section*   (pp. 22–44)

❓ *Alternatively you might be asking:*

But surely we don't need divine help in order to live a good life?   (Turn to p. 167)
But does this 'radical inner change' really happen to people?   (Turn to p. 108)

Jesus and his earliest followers may have been clever frauds

This is not a new idea. And in our day it's been used to launch dozens of lurid paperbacks peddling speculative theories. Take Hugh Schonfield's *The Passover Plot*, for instance, which claims to explain how Jesus planned to fake his own resurrection. Or *The Holy Blood and the Holy Grail*, which asserts that Jesus never died on the cross, but got married, and eventually had descendants who are still alive somewhere on the continent of Europe today. Or Morton Smith's *Jesus the Magician*, which paints a picture of Jesus as a powerful cabbalistic conjuror, his arms tattooed with mystical Egyptian signs, binding his followers to him by repulsive rites of blood sacrifice . . .

This is not the place to answer these theories in detail. (But be assured, it can be done!) The question they all pose is the same: was Jesus a fraud? Well, if he was, I can make only three comments.

First, it doesn't seem to me that the early Christians stood to gain much by their hoaxing. Their message sounded like blasphemy to the Jews and dangerous revolutionary treachery to the Romans. As a strategy for winning friends and influencing people, it left a lot to be desired. There were plenty of better approaches they could have tried if they simply wanted to con people. And predictably, Jesus himself was executed, while most of his inner circle of followers died violent, bloody deaths. Either they were the world's least successful con-men—or martyrs for a cause in which they truly and passionately believed.

Second, the way in which the fraud was perpetrated doesn't seem very clever. Jesus had plenty of chances to win popular support, but he misused them again and again—upsetting influential people, saying such controversial things to a friendly crowd that they all left him and went home, failing to put in an appearance at the most strategic moment to gain maximum publicity . . . A public relations consultant would have had a fit! And if the tales of his miracles and resurrection are inventions, one wonders why the writers didn't bother to rehearse their stories a little better. There are loose ends all over the place, details that don't seem to match up, seeming conflicts of evidence. You can make sense of it, but on the surface it doesn't fit together smoothly.

Third, some of the things which are most undeniable in Jesus' story seem to me to take some explaining, if the man was a fraud. For example, it is overwhelmingly likely that he really did perform miracles (see p. 29). And it can't be denied that his teaching shows a profundity and originality far superior to anything Jewish thinkers had produced for the previous 700 years. Besides, most confidence tricksters win a hearing by the sheer force of their own personalities, but lose their impact rapidly when they're not physically present any more; but it is a matter of simple historic record that when Jesus died he had very few followers. It was shortly afterwards that his massive, revolutionary movement started.

Can you really believe that the man who taught more profoundly about honesty than anyone else in the world's history was actually living a complete lie? That's what you're saying, if you maintain that Jesus was a fraud!

Do you find this a convincing answer?
☐ YES   ☐ NO   ☐ POSSIBLY

If you have further objections to Christian claims about JESUS, read some other parts of this section   (pp. 22–44)

Alternatively you might be asking:

Jesus may have been honest, but isn't the church just a money-spinning racket?   (Turn to p. 71)
But surely Jesus never meant to start the church?
                                                        (Turn to p. 78)

Perhaps Jesus was a lunatic

Well, yes, lunatics often make grandiose claims for themselves. And if Jesus really claimed to be God (see p. 35), the chances are that he was suffering from a kingsize delusion of the most dangerous type. Even Adolf Hitler, even Genghis Khan never made a claim so huge! And wouldn't it be ironic if millions of people over two thousand years had been building their lives around the ravings of a madman?

However, few people have seriously maintained the theory that Jesus was mad. And you can see why, as soon as you look at the Gospels. The teaching of Jesus, as recorded for us there, was clearly original, ethically profound and logically self-consistent. It isn't a matter of isolated flashes of brilliance, such as an unbalanced mind might occasionally be capable of; the whole thing is so carefully developed, so thoughtful and rational, that it is at once apparent that we are in the presence of one of the greatest minds of the ages.

(And it's no use saying that the Gospels may not reflect

Jesus' teaching very accurately. Even if the Gospel writers had got ninety per cent of it wrong—which I don't believe they did, as you'll find on p. 25—enough remains to give us a clear picture of a strikingly intelligent, totally original thinker who couldn't possibly have been 'invented' by the people who happened to write down his sayings. The real Jesus stands out clearly from the pages of the historical record.)

If Jesus had been mad, his disciples would have known. They spent three years in the closest possible contact with him—travelling around the countryside, sleeping rough on many occasions, sharing their food and talking for hours. Often they saw Jesus under pressure, hemmed in by hostile opponents, pursued by sensation-seekers in search of a miracle, hungry, thirsty and tired. But he never cracked under the strain—not once. Had he shown any signs of insanity, they'd have left him straight away. They were good Jews, and in those days Jews believed that anyone who was mad had been accursed by God. You gave lunatics a wide berth.

But obviously the disciples never suspected that their leader was mad. What is more interesting, *nor did anyone else*. On one occasion only did Jesus' enemies try to make this claim—and immediately they were laughed to scorn (John 10:20–1). Writers who were hostile to Jesus accused him of blasphemy, sorcery, all sorts of things—but never of madness, although it would have been a devastating charge to lay. Why did they fail to accuse him of lunacy? Perhaps because they knew it wouldn't sound convincing. People who had met Jesus knew he wasn't mad.

If Jesus was not mad, and if he was not a fraud (see p. 40), that leaves us with a problem. Because Jesus claimed quite clearly to be God (see p. 35)! And 'good men' don't do that sort of thing—so you can't dismiss Jesus by saying, 'Oh, he was just a good man.' He could either be a madman, deluded about his own importance. Or he could be a bad man, fooling the public in order to make money. But if you dismiss those two possibilities, there is only one option left.

Not madman, nor bad man, but God-man . . .

Do you find this a convincing answer?
☐ YES   ☐ NO   ☐ POSSIBLY

!

If you have further objections to Christian claims about JESUS, read some other parts of this section (pp. 22–44). If you have read this whole section, go back to the START HERE page (p. 1) and choose another direction.

?

Alternatively you might be asking:

But how can I be sure it was all true?

(Turn to p. 180)

But how is Jesus so unique—aren't there lots of religions which could just as easily be true as Christianity? (Turn to p. 73)

---

1. John 20:30–31.
2. Rudolf Bultmann, *Jesus and the Word* (London, 1934), 8.
3. Malcolm Muggeridge, *Jesus Rediscovered* (London, 1968), 98.
4. M. E. Osterhaven, 'Sinlessness of Christ', in W. A. Elwell, ed., *Evangelical Dictionary of Theology* (London, 1985), 1018.
5. David Day, *This Jesus . . .* (London, 1980), 40–1.
6. John 21:25.
7. Dale Rhoton, *Can We Know?* (Bombay, 1968), 23.
8. Matthew 10:34–5.

QUESTIONS ABOUT THE BIBLE

You have said that you agree with the statement

I'm not convinced the Bible is trustworthy

This could be your opinion for several reasons. Here are some of the most common reasons people come up with. Tick whichever one(s) may apply to you.

☐ How do we know the right books are in the
  Bible? Some others were suppressed   (p. 46)
☐ The Bible can't be trusted as it is full of errors   (p. 48)
☐ There are so many differences between the
  various manuscripts that we don't know what
  the Bible originally said   (p. 50)
☐ The Bible can be read in different ways; any
  interpretation could be correct   (p. 53)
☐ Some books of the Bible disagree with others   (p. 55)
☐ There are lots of other sacred books—aren't
  they just as valuable?   (p. 57)
☐ Archaeological discoveries have exploded many
  Bible claims   (p. 59)
☐ You can't take the Bible literally today   (p. 61)
☐ It is impossible to live by Bible standards in
  this day and age   (p. 63)
☐ Experience is what counts—any set of words is
  just an inadequate imperfect record   (p. 65)

Now turn to the page(s) in this Section on which the answer is given to the statements you have ticked.

◀ Read them, and decide what you think of the answers
   supplied. Then you can go back to the START HERE page
at the beginning of the book, and choose another direction.

▶   Or if you feel you've surveyed the evidence sufficiently
     already, turn straight to Section 9 (YOURSELF)—on p.
187—and follow the instructions there in order to check out
your own position.

How do we know the right books are in the Bible? Some others were suppressed

'Suppressed' isn't quite the right word—as we'll see in a
moment. But it is certainly true that there were other books
written in the time of the Old Testament and New Testament,
which have been left out of our present Bible. Why is that?

Some people suspect a conspiracy. Erich Von Däniken, for
example—the Swiss author who claims that the human race
was begun by extra-terrestrials as a controlled experiment—
believes that the present Bible was more or less fabricated by a
church council which met centuries after the time of Christ.
Other popular authors have made the same claim.

But there was no conspiracy. The books we have today came
to be recognized by a long, slow process of appreciating their
usefulness and power—not by some arbitrary decree from a
church committee. The Jews never established a council to
debate what should be in the Jewish Scriptures (now the Old
Testament), yet by Jesus' day it was generally agreed what was
inspired and what wasn't. Josephus, the greatest Jewish
historian, could say:

> With us, one does not find innumerable books, mutually
> divergent and conflicting, but only twenty-two, comprising
> the whole past, and in which one is obliged to believe. As so
> much time is already passed now, yet no one of us has ever
> ventured to take anything away from them, or to add
> anything to them, or to make even the slightest alteration.[1]

(Josephus' 'twenty-two' seem to have been identical to the 39
we possess nowadays—it's just that he counted them differently!) As for the books that weren't included, many of
them—the so-called 'Apocrypha' and 'Pseudepigrapha'—are
still in existence today. They were not suppressed; but, as a
quick reading of them will show, although they contain some

good writing they are on a far lower level than the other Scriptures, and it is not hard to see why they were left out.

What about the New Testament? One of the favourite claims of sensational paperback writers is that there were other scriptures which were excluded because they gave away secret information about Jesus which the church wanted to keep quiet. Donovan Joyce wrote about *The Jesus Scroll* (which he claims to have seen, but can't produce); Morton Smith claimed to have traced *The Secret Gospel* (and, again, it can't be made available). Is this true?

The answer has got to be: certainly not. It is true that many other books circulated in the early Christian churches, besides the twenty-seven we now have in the New Testament. But the final choice was not made by any church council. No church council ever debated the contents of the New Testament until the fourth century—and it had all been settled a long time before. 'By the end of the second century,' says Robert Grant, 'there was no longer any question about the core of the New Testament.' All that the fourth century councils were doing was recognizing the list of books which had proved their worth over hundreds of years already.

Books were accepted not because they followed an approved official 'line', but because they came from the teaching of the earliest apostles, who were specially commissioned by Jesus to establish the church's basis of belief. This is why the books started to be collected in the second century: because around 150 AD the apostolic age was coming to an end. 'Until then there were people in places of authority who had known at least one of the Apostles personally,' says scholar Gerald Bray, 'and who had received instruction directly from them. After that, the teaching was second-hand and the need for a recognized canon became much more pressing.'[2] The New Testament came into being not because one bunch of church leaders wanted to impose their views on the rest—but because Christians everywhere were absolutely determined to preserve the original, genuine teaching of Jesus for centuries to come.

Do you find this a convincing answer?
☐ YES ☐ NO ☐ POSSIBLY

| ! | *If you have further objections to the trustworthiness of the BIBLE, read some other parts of this section   (pp. 45–67)* |

If you have further objections to the trustworthiness of the BIBLE, read some other parts of this section   (pp. 45–67)

| ? | *Alternatively you might be asking:* |

But doesn't the Bible present a picture of a God who is
just a bloodthirsty tyrant?   (Turn to p. 12)
But aren't the New Testament stories of Jesus just
biased propaganda documents?   (Turn to p. 25)

(Turn to p. 12)
(Turn to p. 25)

The Bible can't be trusted as it is full of errors

The first thing we need to notice about this objection is that it
assumes that the Bible is a certain kind of book. It assumes the
Bible is more like a telephone directory than a story book. For
it would be a devastating criticism to hold up a telephone
directory and say, 'This book is full of errors!' But if you said
the same thing about (say) one of the 'Postman Pat' books,
nobody would be very impressed.

What's the difference? A telephone directory is a compen-
dium of factual information. A story book uses facts in a rather
different way . . .

Now the Bible does contain a lot of factual information. And
some of it is critically important. For example, if you could
prove that Jesus never lived (see p. 23), or that his teaching
was very different from what the Bible claims, you would have
undermined Christianity completely. But the Bible isn't just an
encyclopaedia of facts. It uses language in many different
ways—and so it is not always appropriate to ask, 'Is this true
or false?'

For a start, there's a lot of figurative language—statements
which are not meant to be taken literally. When the Bible talks
about the eyes of the Lord running throughout the earth, or a
beast with iron teeth and a horn on its head which spoke
boastfully, it's pretty obvious that we are not meant to take

this as literal information! Again, we have to read the statements of the Bible in their context if we are to make sense of them. There's actually one verse which says, 'There is no God!' However, if you read the context, you find the full quotation is, 'The fool has said in his heart, "There is no God" '—quite a different message!

One famous statement about the Bible's inerrancy said this:

> When total precision of a particular kind was not expected nor aimed at, it is no error not to have achieved it. Scripture is inerrant, not in the sense of being absolutely precise by modern standards, but in the sense of making good its claims and achieving that measure of focused truth at which its authors aimed.[3]

In other words, sometimes the Bible isn't trying to be absolutely precise. For instance, the four Gospels sometimes list the events of the life of Jesus in a different order from one another. This isn't a contradiction; it's just that in those days historians weren't concerned with the order of events as much as we are today. Their chief concern was to record that these things happened, and how they took place. An early Christian, Papias, cheerfully explains that Mark took down notes to help him write his Gospel 'not in order', but 'taking care to leave out nothing that he heard and to make no misstatement about it'.

Again, when Jesus began a story, 'A certain man had two sons', he was probably making it up. Howard Marshall comments:

> If the question is asked, 'Is the story true?' the answer probably has to be 'No, it didn't happen like that'. But if in fact the story is a parable, and the appropriate question to ask about a parable is not whether the events described actually happened, but whether the point made by the story is 'true' in the sense of being valid: is it true that God will treat us in the way that the father in the story treated his sons?[4]

When we read the Bible carefully, and ask it the right questions, most of these problems about errors and contradictions disappear very quickly. And in the parts where historical accuracy is absolutely vital, there is breathtaking exactness. We have already noticed what a good historian Luke is (see p. 25); and attempts to find inaccuracies in the Bible have rebounded again and again. (Scholars used to say the Hittites didn't exist, as they couldn't be traced anywhere outside the Bible; and that Pontius Pilate was probably an invention because he didn't appear anywhere else in history; but now we know that the Hittites were one of the biggest Near Eastern civilizations, and that Pontius Pilate definitely did govern Judaea in the reign of Tiberius. Two examples, of thousands.)

No archaeological find has ever disproved a biblical claim. No other ancient source has been so attacked, and so vindicated.

Full of errors? Not likely.

Do you find this a convincing answer?
☐ YES   ☐ NO   ☐ POSSIBLY

If you have further objections to the trustworthiness of the BIBLE, read some other parts of this section   (pp. 45–67).

Alternatively you might be asking:

But surely stories such as the virgin birth are just legendary?   (Turn to p. 31)
If the Bible is true, why hasn't Christianity brought peace to the world?   (Turn to p. 153)

There are so many differences between the various manuscripts that we don't know what the Bible originally said

If you copy out this page, the chances are that you will make at least one mistake before you reach the last line. Human beings are like that. When they get tired, or bored, errors tend to

happen. And if you have a very long book which has been
endlessly copied and re-copied over many centuries, you're
bound to have thousands of mistakes. Aren't you? Well . . .
maybe not.

We don't possess the original manuscripts of the Bible any
more. All we have are copies of copies. And there are 150,000
disagreements between the various manuscripts of the New
Testament which we possess! How could anybody hope to
know what the original said?

Well, first, it isn't surprising that we don't have the originals
any more. The materials used for writing in those days were so
flimsy that they have disintegrated a long time ago, and we do
not have the original of *any* book written in New Testament
times. For most key books of that period you'd expect to find
about nine or ten manuscripts, the earliest of them dating from
about a thousand years after the book was first written.

For Thucydides' *History of the Peloponnesian War*, we have
eight ancient copies. The earliest is from 1300 years after the
book was first written. For Caesar's *Gallic Wars* there are ten
manuscripts, going back to 900 years after Caesar. All this is
quite normal for ancient historical sources. What about the
New Testament?

The answer is staggering. We have about *five thousand*
manuscripts, in whole or in part; and if they all disintegrated
overnight, we'd still be able to reconstitute almost all of the
New Testament, because it's quoted so extensively in early
church writers too! And the earliest *complete* manuscripts of
the New Testament come from around 350 AD. We have
fragments going back much, much further than that.

Now if scholars can claim that we're fairly sure of what
Julius Caesar wrote (and they do), it is obvious that we're on
much surer ground with the New Testament. We are not short
of manuscripts, writes expert Robert Grant; far from it; indeed,
'we have so much that it is very difficult to control'. But wait a
minute. What about those 150,000 differences?

Well, once you have dismissed those which are obviously
wrong readings (because they don't make sense as they
stand), meaningless variations of grammar and word order,
and trivial variations of meaning (where the two alternatives
mean virtually the same thing), you're left with only about

fifty cases where the meaning of the passage is affected in any
way. Most of these can be settled by using our background
knowledge. Of the remaining few, there isn't a single case
where an important doctrine, teaching or story is affected. The
text is almost unbelievably clear.

So much for the New Testament. What about the Old? Well,
we have already quoted a statement by Josephus (see p. 46)
which shows how carefully the Jews looked after their sacred
books. (He adds, 'Time and again ere now the sight has been
witnessed of prisoners enduring tortures and death in every
form in the theatres, rather than utter a single word against
the laws and the allied documents.')

Jewish scribes took immense care to copy their manuscripts
properly. When the Dead Sea Scrolls were discovered in 1948,
all of a sudden we had access to Old Testament manuscripts
which were much older than any we'd seen before. When
these older copies were compared with the more recent ones
we already possessed, an amazing degree of accuracy in
transmission was found.

To say that 'we can't know what the Bible originally said'
isn't an argument. It's just a cop-out.

Do you find this a convincing answer?
☐ YES   ☐ NO   ☐ POSSIBLY

---

*If you have further objections to the trustworthiness of the
BIBLE, read some other parts of this section   (pp. 45–67).*

Alternatively you might be asking:

But couldn't Jesus and his followers have been clever
fraud?   (Turn to p. 40)
But hasn't Jesus' original simple message of love been
distorted?   (Turn to p. 38)

The Bible can be read in different ways; any interpretation could be correct

At the sixteenth century court of the French King Charles IX lived a strange prophet named Nostradamus. He wrote a thousand rhyming quatrains in a strange mixture of French, Greek and Latin, which many people believe contain vital information about the future of mankind. Nostradamus is said to have predicted Hitler, Napoleon and the French Revolution. However, as occultist Peter Underwood admits, his words are 'so deliberately obscure that the texts are difficult to understand even by those who have studied them for years; various interpretations have been made on almost every rhyme'. You can make Nostradamus mean more or less whatever you like.

Many people think that the Bible is like this—an obscure book of dark, difficult riddles, which no-one can really make sense of. Recently I heard Germaine Greer comment on a television programme that the Bible was a 'structure of metaphors' which didn't mean anything directly but just had to be invested with meaning by each succeeding age in its own contemporary terms. If this is true, it means that the Bible is up for grabs. You can use it to back up any point of view you like! But is it true?

The best answer is just to read it for yourself. Anyone who takes the time to flick through Mark, John, or Romans will find that some very clear statements are being made, and some very specific claims are being advanced. It isn't all that difficult. It's logical, and it presents a consistent message— about a God who loves human beings, despite their rebellion against him, and cares for them so much that he made the ultimate sacrifice of taking the punishment they deserved upon himself so as to give them a new life of moral power and closeness to him.

'But,' someone might argue, 'what about all the different denominations? You don't agree with the Mormons or the Jehovah's Witnesses, do you? Yet you all claim to base your beliefs on the Bible!'

This is a fair comment. It's true that there are passages of the Bible which people can have different views about; and it's true that sometimes the Bible does not give a clear, unambiguous ruling on some questions, so that Christians can disagree about minor issues (such as, for instance, whether you should baptize babies or believing adults; or whether communion services should happen every Sunday, or less often; and so on). But on the major issues of belief and conduct, the Bible leaves us in no doubt.

Groups like the Mormons and Jehovah's Witnesses pose a different problem. It isn't really true that they are based on the Bible. The Mormons get very few of their distinctive beliefs from Scripture; in reality they follow the 'revelations' of a nineteenth century prophet who claimed direct inspiration from God. Most of what he says conflicts totally with the Bible (there is no space to argue this here, but you could look at Floyd McElveen's *The Mormon Illusion* (Gospel Light) if you want more facts); and they simply ignore the discrepancies. If there are differences, they claim, it must be that the Bible has been 'incorrectly translated'!

The Jehovah's Witnesses similarly follow just one line of teaching which does not take into account many of the Bible's statements. They refuse to study what the original Bible writers meant, but interpret verses in wildly imaginative ways. (See Anthony Hoekema, *Jehovah's Witnesses* (Paternoster), for a full investigation.)

So don't assume that every group which *claims* to be based on the Bible really is! But whcn people look at the Bible carefully and read it honestly, the message and the challenge it provides is inescapable.

⚖️ *Do you find this a convincing answer?*
   ☐ YES   ☐ NO   ☐ POSSIBLY

❗ *If you have further objections to the trustworthiness of the BIBLE, read some other parts of this section*   (pp. 45–67)

Alternatively you might be asking:

But surely it doesn't matter what you believe as long as you're sincere? (Turn to p. 113)
But if the church was really Christian, would there be so many splits and divisions? (Turn to p. 80)

Some books of the Bible disagree with others

The Bible consists of sixty-six books, written over a period of four thousand years, by about forty authors. Some were kings and others were peasants. Some had a sophisticated education and others had none. It wouldn't be surprising if there were disagreements between them. But if the Bible really is the Word of God, shouldn't all the different books agree with one another? What are the facts?

Really, the amazing thing about the Bible is how much agreement there is. From book to book, the themes that develop and intertwine are consistent and related. The same view of God, the same ideals for human conduct, the same understanding of Jesus and his importance . . . It almost looks miraculous. Which, if Christians are correct in their claims, it is.

That's not to say that there are no differences of style and emphasis. The various authors may have been writing under the influence of the Holy Spirit (see 2 Peter 1:21), but that didn't mean becoming hypnotized zombies, listlessly writing down the words as some supernatural force dictated them. No, all the marks of their own personal, very human style are there. And sometimes that can create *seeming* disagreements which in fact aren't anything of the kind.

One famous example is the difference between Romans 4, which clearly says that Christians are put right by God by *faith* and not *deeds*, and James 2, which seems to say the opposite:

What good is it, my brothers, if a man claims to have faith but has no deeds? Can such faith save him? . . . faith without deeds is useless . . . You see that a person is justified by what he does and not by faith alone.

Paul seems to be saying, 'Faith, not deeds'; James is insisting, 'Deeds, not faith'. But this isn't a real contradiction. If you read enough of both writers, you soon realize that both believe the same thing: faith is what puts people right with God; but a life of good deeds is the only real proof that you actually have any faith! So both things count! It's just that Paul stresses faith—because that's what he's most interested in—whereas James stresses works—which is what *he* really wanted to highlight.

We must recognize that there are one or two places in the Old Testament where different books give accounts of the same military adventures, and the two accounts disagree about the size of the armies involved. (For example, 1,700 horsemen in 2 Samuel 8 become 7,000 horsemen in 1 Chronicles 18.) There are usually good explanations for how these differences crept in; and, anyway, it would be wrong to demand more accuracy from the Bible writers than they really intended to give. None of us is absolutely accurate all the time; if you say to me, 'The sun rises in the east, and goes down in the west', I may notice that absolutely speaking you are uttering scientific nonsense (the sun doesn't 'rise' at all), but I know exactly what you mean. On one level, you're speaking the truth. And, similarly, when the Gospels change the order of events in the life of Jesus (see p. 49), this isn't a serious conflict between them; they're just not too interested in strict chronological accuracy.

You will not find one important instance of disagreement between two books of the Bible. Where you do find small, trifling cases, you're probably looking at minuscule details which the authors weren't concerned to be exact about, because they didn't matter a bit. The Bible speaks with one clear, strong, consistent voice.

Do you find this a convincing answer?
☐ YES   ☐ NO   ☐ POSSIBLY

If you have further objections to the trustworthiness of the BIBLE, read some other parts of this section   (pp. 45–67)

Alternatively you might be asking:

But couldn't some of the other religions be just as true as Christianity?   (Turn to p. 10)
But haven't our communications with the dead disproved the Bible's message anyway? (Turn to p. 121)

There are lots of other sacred books. Aren't they as valuable as the Bible?

The world is full of religious books. And to believers, they can seem the most precious objects on earth. 'Cling to the Bible, though all else be taken,' sing the Christians; while Muslims wrap their copy of the Qur'an in expensive silk and will touch it only after undergoing ritual cleansing; and missionaries from pop Hindu cults sell modern translations of their *bhakti* scriptures on the streets. It prompts the question: aren't all these books on the same level? Why revere the Bible, rather than any of the others?

For the Bible does seem to make arrogantly exclusive claims for itself. It says that God has spoken through the prophets and fathers of the Jewish tradition (Hebrews 1:1–3) and has completed his revelation by sending Jesus. God has nothing more to say. And although the Apostle Paul admitted that the religious quest of other traditions could guide them in the direction of the real God (Acts 17:26–27), the attitude of the biblical writers was uncompromising. Other religions were not paths to God. 'Turn from these worthless things,' Paul cried to a group of pagan worshippers in Lystra; the word he used means 'ineffective, ungrounded, useless, unprofitable'. In one of his letters (Ephesians 2:12) he refers to people who are not Christians as 'without God'—*atheos*, the word from which we derive 'atheist'.

It was the same in the Old Testament. As Christopher Wright points out, the idea of men bowing down to anything other than the God of the Bible 'drew from Old Testament narrators, psalmists and prophets responses varying between incredulity, pity, contempt, indignation, satire, and judgement'. Other religious revelations were non-starters.

Now this is not to say that non-Christian sacred books have no value. They may contain profound human insights, shrewd observations of the nature of things, subtle philosophical reasonings, noble ethical principles. But according to the Bible they're useless to do the one most important thing human beings need—to introduce people to their Maker. Only through Jesus Christ will they be able to form a friendship with him.

The Qur'an contains a forceful picture of God and has a truly impressive moral power. But it shrinks from presenting God as someone with whom human beings can have a relationship of love. Allah is the all-powerful and all-merciful; how could he demean himself to come so close to his creatures? And so we can only be 'Muslim'—the word means 'submissive'. We are to live in obedient fear of God—not the confident friendship of which the Bible speaks.

The great scriptures of Hinduism and Buddhism offer many routes to the knowledge of God. But often it is not clear in Hindu writings whether God is a person who can be known, or just a great force. And the point of life is to lose one's identity, to sink permanently into the cosmic sea—not to share a relationship of love with a God who treats our identity as important.

For the Buddha, the gods were remote beings who were not going to help human beings supernaturally. So Buddhism evolved as a self-help philosophy to enable human beings to make their own way through life without relying on a God who would not reveal himself. Again, the sacred scriptures fail to give us what the Bible considers most valuable.

But is the Bible right? *Can* you have a genuine, unmistakable relationship with God of a kind that transforms your life by its impact? This is the vital question—and you can judge for yourself by reading further in this book. Obviously, if God can be met—and only the Bible contains the secret—the Bible is far more important than any book in the world.

⚖️ *Do you find this a convincing answer?*
☐ YES   ☐ NO   ☐ POSSIBLY

❗ *If you have further objections to the trustworthiness of the BIBLE, read some other parts of this section* (pp. 45–67)

❓ *Alternatively you might be asking:*

But don't all religions lead to God?   (Turn to p. 73)
Are people still experiencing this 'relationship with God', or is the number dropping nowadays?
(Turn to p. 106)

Archaeological discoveries have exploded many Bible claims

'Impossible,' said many scholars. 'Vikings reached America before Columbus? Just a silly myth.'

But then in 1961 archaeologists started to excavate a village in Newfoundland. Sure enough, they discovered a ruined Viking settlement—even a Norse bronze pin. Suddenly the old sagas had 'come true'.

Truth can often be stranger than fiction—as archaeology has demonstrated again and again. Another example is the wealthy city of Spina in northern Italy, referred to by classical authors.

'It never existed,' said the experts. 'Or someone was exaggerating!' Then in 1953 they stumbled upon innumerable tombs packed with all sorts of treasures, and in 1956 aerial photographs confirmed the size and importance of Spina. The experts were wrong again.

Has archaeology destroyed—or confirmed—the Bible's claims? A few years ago, in a television series called *B.C.*, Magnus Magnusson caused a storm by suggesting that the 'historical facts' in the Bible were no more than legends. Many historians reacted angrily; Alan Millard, a prominent British archaeologist, immediately wrote a booklet to defend the Bible; one leading scholar in Birmingham even gave a lecture on 'The Myth of Magnus Magnusson'! But many ordinary people felt Magnusson was confirming what they had always suspected—the Bible was a jumble of myths, legends and fancy stories.

What is the truth?

People often think that the Bible is traditional literature, stories handed down by word of mouth over centuries before they were eventually written down. Not true. Says Alan Millard, 'The major part of biblical history took place in a world where writing was long established and well known, and in a land where it was practised in its easiest form.' It's extremely likely that the historical details were written down almost as they happened—not years afterwards.

And they were written down carefully. It's striking to notice how perfectly the unfamiliar foreign names ('Tiglath-Pileser', 'Nebuchadnezzar') of Assyrians and Babylonians have been preserved in the Bible documents. Obviously the scribes involved had an obsessive concern for accuracy and tremendous pride in their work. It's unlikely that the biblical record has become disfigured by lots of careless errors.

As a result, archaeology has vindicated the Bible's accuracy again and again. The experts said that horses and chariots were unknown in Egypt in the time of Joseph. Then they found some. They claimed that Gallio could never have been procurator of Achaia. Then an excavated slab proved otherwise. They asserted that 'Tirhakah king of Ethiopia' couldn't possibly have led an army in 701 BC, as the Bible claimed, since he was only nine years old. Then an inscription was published which altered their ideas. They said that Belshazzar did not exist outside the Bible, and that he was never king of the Chaldeans. But cuneiform tablets in Babylon prove that he did exist, and did share the kingship with his father Nabonidus.

Need we go on? (For, believe me, we could.) Archaeology is no enemy to the Bible. Quite the reverse!

Do you find this a convincing answer?
☐ YES   ☐ NO   ☐ POSSIBLY

| ! | *If you have further objections to the trustworthiness of the BIBLE, read some other parts of this section* (pp. 45–67) |

| ? | *Alternatively you might be asking:* |

But have we any evidence to prove that Jesus himself existed? (Turn to p. 23)
But surely it's impossible to see any meaningful patterns in history anyway? (Turn to p. 160)

You can't take the Bible literally today

Agreed. As I've already remarked on another page (p. 49), there are many kinds of writing in the Bible. Some of them are supposed to be taken literally; others are not. And if you try to take them literally, you end up making incredible blunders.

Here, for instance, are the first two lines of a famous poem, Shelley's *Ode to a Skylark*:

Hail to, thee, blithe Spirit!
Bird thou never wert.

Rubbish. A skylark is, ornithologically speaking, a bird. But the poet is not trying to propound a new and startling zoological theory here. He's saying something quite different, and for the British Zoological Association to send him stiff letters of reproof would be a totally inappropriate response.

In the same way, you find poetry and imaginative writing in the Bible. And you must not take it literally. When the writer of the *Song of Songs* remarks that his beloved's hair is like a flock of goats descending from Mount Gilead, you mustn't imagine it bleating, jumping, and smelling horrible!

Sometimes Christians disagree over whether certain parts are supposed to be read literally or not. Take, for instance, the story of Jonah—did he really live, or is it fiction? It reads like a fictional story; but then Jesus seems to have believed that Jonah was real. I think he existed, but either way, you may believe in his existence or not and still be challenged just as strongly by the central message of the *Book of Jonah*.

Similarly, we've already seen (p. 9) that Christians disagree about whether the beginning of Genesis is supposed to be a literal account of human origins or not. However they read it, though, the same important, inescapable message comes across: that we are not a chance production, that we are actually made in the image of our creator, and that we are responsible to him for the mess we have made of this planet.

But this doesn't mean that *everything* can be read symbolically or non-literally. There are parts of the Scriptures that make a plain, open claim to be telling the straight facts, and appeal to us to accept them quite literally. Jesus Christ really did live, die, and rise again. He really was the Son of God. There really is a choice to be made in this life which will lead on to a real, inevitable judgement at Jesus' real return. There are definite ways of living in this world which we really must adopt if we want to please God. We are not at liberty to change everything in the Bible to suit ourselves.

'We did not follow cleverly invented stories,' says the *Second Letter of Peter*, 'when we told you about the power and coming of our Lord Jesus Christ.' 'I am not insane, most excellent Festus,' said Paul to a Roman governor. 'What I am saying is true and reasonable.' The early Christians staked all their hopes on the belief that a man really and literally had risen from the dead: 'If Christ has not been raised, our preaching is useless and so is your faith.'[5]

These vital, central claims still need to be 'taken literally' today. In fact, if you don't read them in that way, you'll never make sense of Christianity.

Do you find this a convincing answer?
☐ YES   ☐ NO   ☐ POSSIBLY

If you have further objections to the trustworthiness of the BIBLE, read some other parts of this section   (pp. 45–67)

Alternatively you might be asking:

But doesn't the idea of evolution do away with the need for God? (Turn to p. 9)
But why are there so many splits and divisions in the church? (Turn to p. 80)

It is impossible to live by Bible standards in this day and age

Do you seriously believe it—or is this just a cop-out statement which leaves you free to avoid the moral challenge of the Bible and selfishly live your own way? Forgive me for starting by insulting you, but I've found that the majority of people who make this statement to me have never really seriously considered the possibility that the Bible's ideas on morality might have a place in their lives. They're just too comfortable the way they are!

Anyway, let's assume you're serious in your objection. You may have four different reasons for making it. You may think that the Bible's standards of conduct are too *idealistic*—great in theory, but impossible to live up to. Well, that's true, if we have to struggle to do it by ourselves; but the Bible claims that God can give us a supernatural ability to withstand the toughest of temptations and live a life of new power by surrendering ourselves to the authority of Jesus Christ. (Read about it in Romans 8:1–9, Galatians 5:13–26, or on p. 108).

(By the way, please don't make the mistake of assuming you know what 'Bible standards' are until you've checked carefully. Hindus often criticize Christians for killing animals for food, since the Bible says 'Do not kill'. Surely this is an example of hypocritical believers cheerfully ignoring the commands of their own religion? But when you check, you find that the verse would be better translated 'Do no murder'. It isn't talking about the killing of animals at all.)

You may feel that Bible standards are too *repressive* for the twentieth century. That was certainly the opinion of many people in the sixties, when Christian sexual morality was laughed to scorn in the heyday of the 'permissive society'. But now even *Cosmopolitan* magazine is running articles with titles like 'Why Living Together is a Rotten Idea' and 'The New Chastity: The Right to Say No'. And *Time* magazine proclaimed on its front cover, 'Sex: The Revolution is Over'. Slowly and painfully, thousands of 'liberated' people worldwide have been finding that God's standards are the real way to freedom after all.

You may feel that Bible standards are *outmoded*—that because we know so much more about human motivation and personality today, the Bible's naive and simplistic view of humanity is inadequate. If so, you may well wonder why researchers have found people with a religious faith to be better adjusted and more altruistic than the average person (see p. 103), and why even today prominent scientists and psychologists still build their lives around the teachings of the Bible.

Living, as we do, in a selfish, materialistic, pleasure-mad civilization, where we spend more on bombs every fortnight than it would take to solve the hunger problem for a year, where one marriage in three is currently crashing in flames within ten years of its beginning, where we haven't enjoyed more than fifteen years of peace within the last two thousand —are we really so superior that we can throw away the best guide we have? Or do we need to make the same discovery recorded by some of the earliest followers of Jesus, in the second century AD:

> We who loved more than anything else being men of means, now bring what we have to a common fund and communicate to the needy. We were haters and murderers of one another; and when it came to foreigners with different social customs, we could not make a common home. But now since the revelation of Christ we share the same manner of life, we pray for our enemies and seek to win over those who unjustly hate us.[6]

Do you find this a convincing answer?
☐ YES   ☐ NO   ☐ POSSIBLY

> **!** *If you have further objections to the trustworthiness of the BIBLE, read some other parts of this section* (pp. 45–67)

> **?** *Alternatively you might be asking:*
>
> But surely it's impossible to change yourself in order to please God? (Turn to p. 169)
> Aren't Christian standards in sex and marriage impossible for most people? (Turn to p. 175)

Experience is what counts—any set of words is just an inadequate imperfect record

Which would you rather do—meet the Queen or read about what it's like to meet her? Surely there can't be any substitute for a face to-face encounter. Words can only describe the reality in a secondhand, partial way . . .

And so—some people argue—if God is a person, as the Bible claims, he must reveal himself in personal encounter. Not through the words of a book. The Bible may be a valuable record of how people have met God in the past; but it's just a record—no substitute for the experience of meeting God personally.

There is truth and falsehood in this argument. Yes, God reveals himself personally in people's lives (see p. 97). But the Bible is more than a record of how it has happened in history! Thousands of people have testified that it was through the Bible that God first spoke directly to them and convinced them of his reality. The Bible isn't a dead textbook of religious data, but the means God uses to communicate with us:

The word of God is living and active. Sharper than any

double-edged sword, it penetrates even to dividing soul and spirit, joints and marrow; it judges the thoughts and attitudes of the heart.[7]

It enters into an intimate dialogue with our lives and creates an awareness of what God himself is saying to us.

And it's just as well that this is the case. For if the Bible were merely a catalogue of strange and wonderful experiences that once happened to privileged people, it wouldn't help us a bit. We could only marvel at the stories and wish they would come true for us. But if the Bible itself can make God come alive in our experience, then it ceases to be 'just history' and becomes an exciting practical possibility for ourselves.

Anyway, we need to be careful not to be too dismissive of 'mere words'. They may be no substitute for experience, but as Bible scholar Howard Marshall points out, 'in fact speech is one of the most characteristic activities of persons by means of which personal relationships are made possible'. Suppose that a soldier falls into enemy hands, and then from the prison camp is able to smuggle a message out to his wife, assuring her that he is alive and well, and still loves her.

> She would not have wanted to say that it was impersonal and that nothing but a personal meeting with her husband would do. Nor could the message and the concern which it embodied have been conveyed in any other way than by words . . . Words are essential and words suffice . . . In short, to say that God cannot make use of words and statements to reveal himself is to go against all that we know of persons and how they relate to one another.[8]

This is why the Old Testament prophets begin their words again and again with 'Thus saith the Lord!' They knew that God was speaking directly through them. And that when their words were written down, God would still speak through them. And also that he would continue to speak through them as long as they were preserved and read.

Do you find this a convincing answer?
☐ YES ☐ NO ☐ POSSIBLY

!

If you have further objections to the trustworthiness of the BIBLE, read some other parts of this section (pp. 45–67). If you have read this whole section, go back to the START HERE page (p. 1) and choose another direction.

?

Alternatively you might be asking:

But isn't this 'experience of God' just a psychological trick? (Turn to p. 92)
If God wants us to believe in him, wouldn't it be more effective to make himself visible? (Turn to p. 16)

---

1. Flavius Josephus, *Contra Apionem*, i.8.
2. Gerald Bray, *Creeds, Councils and Christ* (Leicester, 1984), 45.
3. Chicago Statement on Biblical Inerrancy. See I. H. Marshall, *Biblical Inspiration* (London, 1982), 49–74.
4. I. H. Marshall, *op. cit.*, 55.
5. 2 Pet. 1:16; Acts 26:25; I Cor. 15:14.
6. The anonymous *Letter to Diognetus*.
7. Hebrews 4:12.
8. I. H. Marshall, *op. cit.*, 15.

QUESTIONS ABOUT THE
CHURCH

You have said that you agree with the statement

I don't like what I've seen of the Church

This could be your opinion for several reasons. Here are some of the most common reasons people come up with. Tick whichever one(s) may apply to you.

☐ The church is a device used by the rich to
  oppress the poor   (p. 69)
☐ The church is just a money-spinning racket   (p. 71)
☐ All religions lead to God; the church has no
  monopoly   (p. 73)
☐ I can worship God without needing to belong
  to a church   (p. 75)
☐ Jesus never meant to start an organization   (p. 78)
☐ If the church was really Christian, there
  wouldn't be so many splits and divisions   (p. 80)
☐ Christianity has been starting wars for
  centuries   (p. 81)
☐ There are too many hypocrites in the church   (p. 84)
☐ The church has always been unfair to women   (p. 85)
☐ What the church does is boring and outdated   (p. 88)

---

*Now turn to the page(s) in this Section on which the answer
is given to the statements you have ticked.*

◀ Read them, and decide what you think of the answers
  supplied. Then you can go back to the START HERE page
at the beginning of the book, and choose another direction.

▶ Or if you feel you've surveyed the evidence sufficiently
already, turn straight to Section 9 (YOURSELF)—on p.
187—and follow the instructions there in order to check out
your own position.

The church is a device used by the rich to oppress the poor

> The rich man in his castle,
>   The poor man at his gate,
> God made them high and lowly
>   And ordered their estate

Not many people sing that verse of 'All things bright and
beautiful' any more; it's too embarrassing. But when the hymn
was first written, a hundred years ago, many Christians felt
quite complacently happy about it. God had made some rich,
and others poor, and that was that. If you didn't have much
money, God obviously intended it that way . . .

One observer at the turn of the century was scathing about
what he called 'suburban religion'. 'It upholds a decent life and
a clean moral standard, with much individual personal piety.
But it is far too content to limit its outlook to its own family or
church . . . It regards with disapproval and often with
contempt this world of poverty with its dumb demand for aid;
it is generous in charity, but no appeal for justice in the name
of the forgotten poor goes forth with united voice from the
churches of South London.'[1] Worse, religion could even be
used as an instrument of social control—to provide moral
backing to the capitalist bosses' exploitation of their work
force. No wonder that when Karl Marx saw middle-class
chapels with pews reserved for the wealthy, prosperous
churchmen living in comfort a few miles away from massive
social problems, and preachers exhorting the humble poor to
be honest and industrious (while no one criticized the
rapacious industrialist)—no wonder that he created the phrase
'opium for the people'.

But is this all that Christianity amounts to—an ideology of oppression? And must it always be that way? Marxists would say 'Yes'; religion is an instrument of repressive inhumanity wielded by economic exploiters. But then Marxists haven't built 85% of the hospitals in the world. Christians have. And Elizabeth Fry, St. Francis and the Earl of Shaftesbury weren't Marxists. They were Christians.

The earliest Christians transformed the society they lived in (see p. 72). They had no time for oppression and injustice. And they were simply living out the pattern left by Jesus Christ:

> My brothers, as believers in our Glorious Lord Jesus Christ, don't show favouritism . . . Has not God chosen those who are poor in the eyes of the world to be rich in faith and to inherit the kingdom he promised those who love him? But you have insulted the poor. Is it not the rich who are exploiting you?[2]

These ideas of equality went right back to the Old Testament, where God established an economic system for the Israelites which was designed to stamp out inequality and assert the importance of the individual. And when the Israelites strayed from it, the prophets were there to denounce fiercely their inhumanity and remind them of God's concern for social justice.

Real Christianity actually has a tremendous record of social concern, self-sacrifice and heroic efforts to bring about fairness for all. Martin Luther King was a clergyman. Both Evangelicals and Catholics played a major role in the peaceful overthrow of the tyrannical Marcos regime in the Philippines, and the downfall of apartheid in South Africa. Slavery vanished from both the Roman empire and also the Western world as a result of the determined efforts of men who took the Bible seriously. And so one could go on multiplying examples.

Yes, Christianity has been misused. Yes, it has sometimes been turned into a haven for the smug and snobbish. But don't confuse the fake with the real. The real is dynamite.

Do you find this a convincing answer?
☐ YES   ☐ NO   ☐ POSSIBLY

If you have further objections to the CHURCH as you've seen it, read some other parts of this section (pp. 68–90)

Alternatively you might be asking:

But isn't Christianity just pie in the sky when you die?
(Turn to p. 149)
But don't people become Christians out of a selfish fear of hell fire? (Turn to p. 104)

The church is just a money-spinning racket

There can be no doubt that some people have made a lot of money out of Christianity. Mediaeval popes with their palaces, mistresses, and art treasures; insincere evangelists of the 'Elmer Gantry' type, jetting around the world in expensive Italian suits; commercial promoters of religious objects and sacred relics—the list is long and dishonourable. And it's not surprising. Whenever people believe strongly in something, they make themselves vulnerable to being ripped off. No wonder shady dealers and unscrupulous exploiters cluster round religions like flies round a honeypot. The pickings are easy.

But does that mean 'the church is *just* a money-spinning racket'? You might think so, as you fend off appeals from Save-the-Steeple funds, pay extortionate prices to look round cathedrals, read scandalous revelations about dishonest vicars' private lives in the *Sunday Sport*. However, there's another side to it.

Consider this: nobody forges nine pound notes. It isn't worth anybody's while to make fake versions of something which doesn't exist. The only objects which do get faked are those which are genuine and valuable! Maybe if there are fake versions of Christianity in existence, there is also a real thing which is being copied . . .

When Christianity began, it most definitely was not a

moneyspinning racket. If you wanted to take money from pious Jews, the last story you should have tried out on them would have been the story that you were the Son of God. That kind of claim wasn't commercially viable; in fact, it was a surefire way of committing suicide by arranging your own execution.

Nor was it a good selling proposition in the Roman Empire to claim that your leader was 'the Lord'. That sounded very like treason. And Christians died heroically, in large numbers, because they wouldn't relinquish this claim. A money-spinning racket?

History is full of examples of sacrificial living by Christians, identifying with the oppressed, sharing their resources, working for the underprivileged. When plague hit the city of Carthage in the fourth century AD, the local bishop,Cyprian, refused to let his people flee. Instead the Christians stayed to tend the sick whom no one else would touch. Because of their courageous stand, they became known as the *'parabolani'*—the gamblers.

And the impact of the early Christians on the Roman empire was outstanding. They gave money and supplies to the needy, widows and orphans. They established hospitals. They visited prisoners and slaves in the mines and provided practical help. They helped to bury the poor, whose relatives couldn't afford a funeral. Church funds were used to ransom slaves. They provided trade training and created work for the unemployed. They campaigned against easy abortion, infanticide, suicide and the cruel gladiatorial games. W. E. H. Lecky, the historian, was not a Christian, but he admits that Christianity was

> . . . a movement of philanthropy which has never been paralleled or approached in thepagan world. The effects of this movement in promoting happiness have been very great. Its effect in determining character has probably been greater still.[3]

And today? Christians are still involved in countless projects of relief and development around the world. Without Christian schools, hospitals, agricultural projects, political action groups, literacy schemes, and a million other things, the world would be in much more of a mess than it is.

If you dismiss Christianity as 'just a money-spinning racket', you haven't even started to examine the facts.

⚖️ *Do you find this a convincing answer?*
  ☐ YES   ☐ NO   ☐ POSSIBLY

❗ *If you have further objections to the CHURCH as you've seen it, read some other parts of this section*   (pp. 68–90)

❓ *Alternatively you might be asking:*

But aren't Christians obsessed with saving their own souls at the expense of the world?   (Turn to p.173)
Isn't religion just a distraction when we have bigger problems to solve?   (Turn to p.157)

All religions lead to God; the church has no monopoly

At the headquarters of the United Nations in New York there is a Meditation Room, 'a room of quiet where only thoughts should speak'. It has been left deliberately bare, so that people of all religions can use it equally, to worship 'the God whom man worships under many names and in many forms'. Said Dag Hammarskjold, Secretary General, 'It is for those who come here to fill the void with what they find in their centre of stillness.'

Is this the way ahead for world religions? Should they merge their identities, drop their distinctive doctrines, and simply realize that everyone is worshipping the same God? Is there any point in staying divided when really all religions lead to God?

It's an attractive thought—on the face of it. If different

religions are just attempts to locate God inside our 'centre of stillness', why can't they all be one?

But wait a minute. At least one major religion—Christianity—claims strongly that God *isn't* inside our 'centre of stillness' (whatever that may be—but then that's another question). Christians claim that humans are naturally cut off from God by the evil in human nature. That the only way for people to contact God is for someone to deal with the problem of evil for us. And that only one person, Jesus Christ, was ever able to do that. So only Christianity can lead us to a true relationship with God. The other faiths are doomed to failure before they start, because they assume that God is somewhere within—and he isn't.

Another problem. When you say that 'all religions' lead to God, what exactly are you including? As William James showed many years ago in his famous *Varieties of Religious Experience*, it's very difficult sometimes to decide what is and isn't a real religion. Are you including in 'all religions' faiths such as Satanism? Faiths that involve human sacrifice and ritual child slaughter? The sick sadism of the Charles Manson cult and the mind-bending techniques of David Koresh who persuaded his followers that all the women should sleep with him, and the entire group should die fighting for him, in his Waco fortress in 1992? 'All religions lead to God'? Really?

In fact, if all religions do lead to God, three things follow which aren't so attractive. First, *none of them tell us anything worth knowing*. Because they all disagree on the most basic points! Some say God's a person; others that there are many gods; others that God is just an impersonal force. Some say we live once, and then are judged; others say we come back for life after life. Some claim this world is real; others claim that 'reality' is just an illusion. If all these religions really have an equal claim to be believed, in fact they cancel one another out, and we're no wiser than when we started.

Second, if all religions lead to God, *God can't care very much about us, or he'd have made his signals a little more clear*. What kind of God allows this sort of confusion to continue—allowing the Hindus to believe one thing, the Muslims another, the Christians another, and all of them to fight and argue about it? Isn't it more believable that, if God truly does care about us, he would make himself clear once and for all, in one conclusive revelation, rather than spreading wild rumours around the planet? And in fact this is exactly what the Bible says did happen:

> In the past God spoke to our forefathers through the prophets at many times and in various ways, but in these last days he has spoken to us by his Son . . . The Son is the radiance of God's glory and the exact representation of his being . . .[4]

Finally, if all religions lead to God, *Christianity is automatically excluded*, because it claims uniqueness for itself. 'I am the way and the truth and the life,' announced Jesus. 'No one comes to the Father except through me.' Either you dismiss his claim as an arrogant lie, and forget about Christianity; or else you start to consider the possibility that just maybe, in this one way, God did give the ultimate revelation of himself to human beings. There is no third option available.

Do you find this a convincing answer?
☐ YES   ☐ NO   ☐ POSSIBLY

If you have further objections to the CHURCH as you've seen it, read some other parts of this section   (pp. 68–90)

Alternatively you might be asking:

But surely Christians are no better than other people?
(Turn to p. 95)
But surely Jesus himself never claimed to be more than a human teacher?   (Turn to p. 35)

I can worship God without needing to belong to a church

Religion used to be what brought people together. Churches, temples and synagogues were packed for services. The religious building used to be the centre of the community—the meeting point, the gossip exchange centre, sometimes the school and the hospital too. Now all that has changed; we've become a much more private society. We would rather stay at home and watch the hymn singing on television. This morning's *Daily Mail* has an article about the decline of chapels in Wales: 4,500 in the year 1900 have dwindled to only 500 now.

As a result, many people reject the idea that you need to go to church in order to worship God. 'I can appreciate him much better in the open air,' they say. 'You can worship God on your own in the countryside much better than in a stuffy church.'

I wonder just how many people who go out for a Sunday run in the country do actually spend any time worshipping God. But never mind. Is the objection valid anyway?

Certainly it isn't churchgoing which makes you a Christian. You may attend a church all your life, sing in the choir, hand out the hymnbooks, teach in the Sunday school, and still not be a Christian. The New Testament constantly exhorts those who belong to churches to be absolutely sure that they really are Christians. 'Examine yourselves, to see whether you are in the faith; test yourselves.' 'See to it, brothers, that none of you has a sinful, unbelieving heart that turns away from the living God.' It isn't how you spend your Sundays, but where your heart is, that decides whether or not you are a Christian (more about this on p. 97).

And, sadly, some churches are not very special. Some are dreary places with little life and vigour, which wouldn't help anyone get more excited about his faith. But that's no excuse for writing them *all* off.

In fact, when you become a Christian, you automatically become part of the church too. The Bible makes this clear. The two things are tied together and can't be separated:

> Consequently, you are no longer foreigners and aliens, but fellow-citizens with God's people and members of God's household . . . you too are being built together to become a dwelling in which God lives by his Spirit.[5]

It should be natural for Christians to be together. The writer of Hebrews ends a long discussion of what it means to be a Christian—having your sins completely forgiven by the sacrifice of Jesus' life—by saying, 'Therefore, brothers . . . let us not give up meeting together, as some are in the habit of doing, but let us encourage one another.'

Why is this? Because Christians need one another. They can give one another help, encouragement and support; on their own, they might be tempted to give it all up in despair. They can stretch and challenge one another, and bring the best out of each other; on your own, you can become fat, selfish and lazy. They can learn how to grow in love and sensitivity to one another; on your own, you'd miss all the richness of this. And they can contribute something valuable to each other. The New Testament says that all Christians have 'spiritual gifts', abilities which God has given them to use for the benefit of others. When we use our 'gifts',

> Just as each of us has one body with many members, and these members do not all have the same function, so in Christ we who are many form one body, and each member belongs to all the others. We have different gifts, according to the grace given to us.[6]

If you try to worship God without belonging to a church, you may just manage to hang on to some sort of impoverished Christian experience. But you'll miss out on the true variety and excitement of real Christian living. That comes to you only through other people.

Do you find this a convincing answer?
☐ YES ☐ NO ☐ POSSIBLY

If you have further objections to the CHURCH as you've seen it, read some other parts of this section (pp. 68–90)

Alternatively you might be asking:

But are people today still becoming Christians, or is the whole thing dying out? (Turn to p.106)
Can I be a Christian without looking like an artificial clone of all the other Christians? I know some that I don't want to be like! (Turn to p. 182)

Jesus never meant to start an organization

By any reckoning, the followers of Jesus Christ have made a sizeable impact on world history. At the beginning of the 1980s, 1,432,686,500 people claimed to be part of the Christian church—and that's a third of the world's population. Over the previous ten years, more than 10,000 'para-church' organizations (missions, relief agencies, publishing houses, and the like) were founded to serve the growing movement. The colossal bureaucracy involved in running something as sizeable as the Roman Catholic Church, or the World Council of Churches, is staggering to behold. But did Jesus Christ ever intend this to happen? If the Galilean preacher came back today, would he be puzzled by all that's happened in his name?

John Lennon of the Beatles once said, 'Jesus was all right, but his disciples were thick. It's them being thick that spoils it for me.' A lot of people are drawn to the quiet, commanding figure of Jesus—but repelled by all the commercialism and ballyhoo that goes on around his church. Did Jesus mean it to be this way? Did he plan to start an organization?

It's certainly true that not everything the church does would win Jesus' approval. The church is made up of erring human beings, and because it is a human structure occasionally the wrong people may end up in charge of it, and occasionally people within it do wild, silly, immoral and hurtful things. Jesus would not have approved of Calvin's burning of his heretical opponents. Or the sickening sham of the Crusades. Or the financial greed of some Popes and cardinals. But that doesn't mean Jesus wouldn't have approved of the church's existence.

Granted, Jesus left very few instructions about how he wanted his followers to organize themselves, and their earliest groups were formed on the pattern of the Jewish synagogue —since that was the kind of organization they already knew. But Jesus did clearly expect his followers to be together, in order to perform certain tasks. They were to tell the world his message. They were to 'make disciples' out of people of all nations. They were to demonstrate that they belonged to Jesus by the special quality of love they would show to one another (John 13:35). Without some kind of structure to hold them together, none of this could be achieved.

He had already groomed his closest followers for positions of leadership, by developing an especially close training relationship with twelve of them (and an even closer relationship with three of that group). He had taught them principles of leadership which were supposed to govern their conduct in his absence (Luke 22:25–6). He left behind a group of people whom he had prepared for responsibility.

When a Jewish rabbi took on some trainees as his disciples, it was usually understood that they would be with him only for a limited period. After about three years, they would 'graduate' and go off to teach what they had learned. But Jesus made it clear to his disciples that once they had joined him they were with him for life. There was no end to following Jesus.

So it would be wrong to see Jesus as a simple, impractical hippy teacher, vaguely scattering bright thoughts and new ideas with no intention of starting a movement. His call to men and women was clear and specific: to join together with him in founding a group that would one day change the world.

Do you find this a convincing answer?
☐ YES   ☐ NO   ☐ POSSIBLY

If you have further objections to the CHURCH as you've seen it, read some other parts of this section   *(pp. 68–90)*

Alternatively you might be asking:

Most of your ideas here are taken from the Gospels —but can they be trusted as information sources?
(Turn to p. 25)
Isn't it possible that Jesus and his earliest followers were merely clever frauds?   (Turn to p. 40)

If the church was really Christian, there wouldn't be so many splits and divisions

It has been estimated that there are more than 21,780 sects and denominations within the Christian church. That's an awful lot of warring points of view. Just over the last year, in my own town, one minister has fallen out with his congregation and left to start a new church; one family has left our own church because of disagreements; and another new group has moved into the town, to begin operations in competition with the fifty or so churches that already exist. If they're all Christians, why on earth can't they all agree?

Well, on another page we make the point (see p. 84) that Christians don't pretend to be perfect. Christians are as liable to make mistakes, lose their temper, and do unworthy things, as anyone else in the population. The only difference is that Christians have admitted their failures to God and are actively allowing him to remodel their lives. So it's unrealistic to expect churches to be model communities of faultless, saintly people.

Splits and divisions in the church are no new thing. Most of the letters in the New Testament were written to churches where squabbles were going on! And the New Testament writers obviously expected Christians to have problems with one another—judging by the emphasis they place upon such qualities as 'longsuffering', 'patience', 'gentleness'. There would be no need for these virtues if the church was a perfect place!

In fact, all religions tend to have these divisions. Nothing uglier has happened between rival groups of Christians than has happened between the Sunnis and Shi'ites in Islam. Fringe groups like the Baha'is and Ahmaddiya have been persecuted by brother Muslims. Between the two wings of world Buddhism, Theravada and Mahayana, there is a profound philosophical divide. Personalists and impersonalists within Hinduism exchange bitter insults. Human beings are the same everywhere . . .

And it would be wrong to assume that because Christians wear different labels and attend different churches, they can't get on. Looking at my diary, so far this year I have worked with Anglicans, Baptists, Methodists, Pentecostals, Catholics, Mennonites and Strict Baptists; with members of the Church of Scotland, the Brethren, house churches, the Salvation Army, and the United Evangelical Church of Poland! And it's only May!

What unites Christians is not an identical outlook on doctrinal matters, or membership of the same group of churches. What forms genuine, invisible bond between real Christians is their uncompromising commitment to follow Jesus Christ, and the experience of new life they have received from him. Everything else is secondary. And once you've experienced the love of Christ creating a supernatural bond between yourself and people who are totally unlike you in every way—you start to realize just how real the new life is!

Do you find this a convincing answer?
☐ YES   ☐ NO   ☐ POSSIBLY

If you have further objections to the CHURCH as you've seen it, read some other parts of this section   *(pp. 68–90)*

Alternatively you might be asking:

But do we need God in order to live a good life and love others?   (Turn to p. 167)
Do people really change at a deep level as a result of becoming Christians?   (Turn to p. 108)

Christianity has been starting wars for centuries

It was the morning of the Battle of Grunwald. The Polish princes and generals had already been to Mass to pray to God for victory in their defence of their homeland. Now they lined up nervously to face the might of the Teutonic Knights . . . And soon over the hill they came, at full tilt, lances raised, bellowing their battle cry.

'Christ is risen! Christ is risen!'

It's a ridiculous picture, isn't it? Two 'Christian' armies fighting one another in the name of God. And it's been repeated many times since. The amount of blood spilt in the Crusades, the sixteenth century wars of religion, and the mediaeval campaigns against heretics, makes for a grim total. In the name of Jesus innocent Jews were massacred in twelfth century England. Aztecs died at the hands of alien oppressors in South America, hosts of innocent people were burned at the stake or stretched on the rack. What a record for the religion of love and human kindness!

But be careful how you criticize. For one thing, not everyone who claims to be 'Christian' actually is. The Jewish massacres had more to do with money than faith; some of the English nobles were hopelessly in debt to Jewish moneylenders, and a righteous campaign to exterminate them neatly solved the financial problem. The Teutonic Knights were a greedy bunch of land-grabbers, who had managed to convince the Pope that the Poles were heathens simply so that they could extend their empire eastwards. Christianity has been an excuse for a war many times; but less often the reason for one.

Not many of those who have thrown petrol bombs or 'kneecapped' informers in Northern Ireland have actually been real Christians. In fact, there is a sizeable group of ex-paramilitary fighters who have actually become Christians and as a result renounced their life of violence. Similarly, in Beirut the 'Christian' armies were not made up of believing adherents of the faith. Real Christians there were actively working for peace and reconciliation.

It's not surprising that people should use Christianity as a ready excuse to start a war, because anything that people feel deeply and believe strongly about provides a good pretext for beginning an argument. So many people have died in the name of Christianity? Well, millions more have died in the name of politics—another major cause of wars—but that doesn't make politics bad or unnecessary.

And Christianity has brought peace as well as conflict.

When a person's life is altered by exposure to Jesus Christ, he can't remain the same. Take Caesar Molebatsi as an example of that; lame since his teenage years as a result of being deliberately run over by a white driver, his heart should be filled with hate for the white racist bigots of his native South Africa. Instead, he's a clergyman in Soweto, and worked for years against official harrassment and the distrust of his own people to bring understanding and reconciliation. I think as well of a young Solidarity fighter I met in Poland some years ago. When he became a Christian, he still wanted justice and free trade unions in his country. But the desperate violence and crippling malevolence were gone. He was a new person in Jesus Christ.

Christians have never found it easy to obey Jesus' command, 'Love your enemies and pray for those who persecute you.' Sometimes even real Christians have become involved in horrific, ghastly acts of inhumanity; because, as we've already seen (p. 80), Christians are not perfect beings, just failures who have admitted it. But the record of Christians as peacemakers in history is second to none. And in their relationship with Jesus Christ they have access to a transforming supernatural love which can help them live completely altered lives.

⚖️ *Do you find this a convincing answer?*
☐ YES ☐ NO ☐ POSSIBLY

❗ *If you have further objections to the CHURCH as you've seen it, read some other parts of this section* (pp. 68–90)

❓ *Alternatively you might be asking:*

Why hasn't Christianity brought peace to the world? (Turn to p. 153)
If God was really there, wouldn't he stop people fighting? (Turn to p. 143)

There are too many hypocrites in the church

There certainly are a lot of hypocrites in the church. People go to church for all sorts of reasons: to impress the neighbours, to cultivate the boss, to hunt down a husband, to compensate for loneliness. But then they go to football matches, or the pub, for all these reasons too. Have you ever heard anybody say, 'I'm not going down to the pub any more because they're all hypocrites down there. They're not really interested in beer'?

Maybe the problem is that we feel sincerity is a lot more important where religion is concerned. But then Christians in a church aren't saying, 'Look at me, I'm perfect!' Belonging to a church is really a way of telling the world: 'Look at me, I'm a failure. I can't live life successfully with only my own resources. I hereby admit that I need God's help not to make a mess of my life.' David Watson put it like this:

> The best definition of the Church I know is that it is 'Christ's hospital'. If I visit a hospital which claims to heal sick people, and I find it full of sick people, I do not say 'What a wretched hospital! What hypocrisy!' Instead, I am glad to know that it is in touch with the right people. Likewise the Church is a fellowship of sinners. If its members are still morally and spiritually sick in various degrees, it is not a denial of the truth of the Christian faith, but only that the Church is in touch with the right people.[7]

And so going to church is not a proclamation of virtue, but a confession of need. Hypocrisy isn't involved unless the person concerned is flaunting his church attendance as a badge of status; but the Bible makes it clear that God is not impressed with that sort of behaviour anyway (look at Jesus' story in Luke 18:9–14). *Nobody* was more scathing about religious hypocrites than Jesus himself.

Two other points you might like to think about. First, honesty about ourselves is something that we all have to learn slowly. It doesn't come naturally, but only as successive layers of illusion are stripped away from us bit by bit. We're all at various stages on the journey between hypocrisy and openness. People in churches are no different—except that Christians have Jesus to guide them gently in the direction of ever-increasing honesty.

And, second, it's easier harbouring grand illusions about yourself when you never expose your personality to contact with other people. Especially those people you wouldn't naturally want to have much to do with. But you learn a great deal about yourself in the cut and thrust of daily dealings with other human beings. And that is what belonging to a church plunges you into. So, judge for yourself—is it easier to be a hypocrite in a church, or in a bedsit?

Do you find this a convincing answer?
☐ YES ☐ NO ☐ POSSIBLY

If you have further objections to the CHURCH as you've seen it, read some other parts of this section (pp. 68–90)

Alternatively you might be asking:

But isn't it impossible to make yourself a better person in order to please God? (Turn to p. 169)
But surely some people are the religious sort, and some are not? (Turn to p. 99)

The church has always been unfair to women

The Christian church—let's face it—is one of the most male-dominated organizations on earth. Many churches will not allow women to be in a position of leadership, and some appeal to the New Testament for their justification for doing so. Jesus Christ was a man, and so were his twelve closest associates. God is usually referred to as 'He' and 'Father'. And throughout history, many church leaders have made statements about the place of women which have been patronising and dismissive.

St. Thomas Aquinas, for example, considered that a girl baby was a defective human being. Tertullian wrote, 'You are the devil's gateway . . . you are the first deserter of the divine law.' Martin Luther had no time for 'all who despise the female sex', but nonetheless had strong views about woman's place: 'A woman does not have complete mastery over herself. God so created her body that she should be with a man and bear and raise children.'

No wonder that feminist Kate Millett has concluded, 'Patriarchy has God on its side.' Christianity diminishes women. The church is unfair to the female. Isn't that so?

Not necessarily. For a start, other religions have said much harsher things about women. (The Qur'an advises husbands, 'As for those from whom you fear disobedience, admonish them and send them to beds apart and beat them.') Some of the attitudes of church leaders have been shaped less by the Bible than by Greek philosophers like Aristotle and Plato, who had little time for women. Jesus' own attitude to women was revolutionary. And as a result, although women have certainly not been treated fairly by men throughout the whole of church history, there has been a certain amount of freedom within Christianity which has allowed great women to appear and to stamp their impression upon their age (Catherine Booth, Elizabeth Fry, Teresa of Avila) in a way which has just not happened in non-Christian cultures.

Jesus grew up in a society where women were undervalued and mistreated. A woman's testimony had no value in a court of law. A woman was not to be educated—'If any man gives his daughter a knowledge of the Law it is as though he taught her lechery'. An ancient Jewish prayer runs, 'Blessed art thou, 0 Lord . . . who hast not made me a woman.' Strict Rabbis would neither talk to nor look at a woman.

Jesus scandalized his religious critics by counting women as well as men among his followers. He not only talked to them and taught them, but treated them as of equal value to the men. Women, like men, were capable of making decisions and were responsible before God for their individual conduct. The first witness of the resurrection was a woman.

So it is not surprising that early Christians believed in the equality of women. 'There is neither male nor female,' taught the Apostle Paul, 'for you are all one in Christ Jesus.' Women in the early church were able to take part in worship, to help in presenting the Christian message to outsiders, to take on a wide range of responsibilities. And all this is a much more male chauvinist society than ours! 'In fact,' reflects Mary Evans, 'in almost every church of which we have details, women were prominent among the nucleus of believers and often played a definite part in leadership.'

Since then the church has not always been good at working out Jesus' revolutionary principle of the equality of men and women. In our own day there are lots of unsettled debates about the place of women in the church. But historically, women have had more respect and freedom under Christianity than under any other religious system. And it is the Christian tradition in the West which has brought about today's concern for the 'liberation' of women.

The church has sometimes been unfair to women; Jesus never was; and his followers today have the chance to demonstrate that in following him all human beings—women as well as men—can find a personal fulfilment they will never find anywhere else.

Do you find this a convincing answer?
☐ YES ☐ NO ☐ POSSIBLY

If you have further objections to the CHURCH as you've seen it, read some other parts of this section (pp. 68–90)

Alternatively you might be asking:

But aren't Christian ideas of sex and marriage hopelessly outmoded and impractical? (Turn to p. 175)
Is it possible to live by Bible standards in this day and age? (Turn to p. 63)

What the church does is boring and outdated

Correction. What *some* churches do is boring and outdated. But you can't generalize. If you go to a steak bar and they serve you a piece of glamourized gristle which is totally inedible, that's sad, but you would be silly to avoid restaurants for the rest of your life. There are good places as well as bad.

Why do so many people who have never been inside a church for years have the firmly fixed idea that 'churches are boring'? One reason has got to be that churches have had a thoroughly bad press. The timid, unworldly, effeminate minister is a stock figure of fun in situation comedies. TV religion is often geared to the elderly and ultra-conservative. When a priest runs off with a choir member, it's instant news; but when the church does something genuinely creative and exciting, the papers rarely report it.

There is nothing 'boring and outdated' about Spring Harvest, a non-stop teaching holiday which happens every Easter when thousands of British Christians from all sorts of denominations take over a holiday camp and have fun while they worship and learn together. Or the Greenbelt Arts Festival, a four-day celebration of Christian creativity in rock music, drama, dance, the visual arts, and every other medium conceivable. There is nothing 'boring and outdated' about the services of St Aldates in Oxford or Eden Baptist Church in Cambridge, where hundreds crowd together each Sunday for the most thrilling few hours of their week. At the other end of the scale, there was nothing 'boring and outdated' about the two tiny house churches I visited earlier this year, where one or two Christians in an informal atmosphere have started to build a new Christian community together.

When thousands of evangelical Christians mass together in peaceful demonstration at barricades in the Philippines, there is nothing 'boring and outdated' going on. When a handful of Chinese young people meet together in the forest early in the morning, so that they can worship God undisturbed, there's plenty of danger but little risk of boredom. Standing for Christ

in Bosnia or Peru or North Africa is not easy, but rarely boring.
Don't write off the church before you've explored the reality.

One reason that so many Westerners find the church
'boring' is that they have completely misunderstood what it is
for. The church is not a celestial entertainment, a sacred
cabaret that unfolds before you as you lounge in your pew.
Viewed simply as a means of entertainment, it leaves a lot to
be desired—that's true; but the church is not a show put on for
the benefit of its customers. It is, in the words of Archbishop
William Temple, 'the only society on earth which exists for the
benefit of its non-members'. It is a place where people can
commit themselves together to hard work—to learning to live
in love with one another, to sharing Christ's love with a
hungry world, to offering new life to broken men and women,
to working for justice and freedom and equality for all
humanity.

Demanding? Certainly. Entertaining? Not always. But
boring? You must be joking.

Do you find this a convincing answer?
☐ YES   ☐ NO   ☐ POSSIBLY

*If you have further objections to the CHURCH as you've seen
it, read some other parts of this section (pp. 68–90). If you
have read this whole section, go back to the START HERE
page (p. 1) and choose another direction.*

Alternatively you might be asking:

But don't Christians all look and behave alike? I
couldn't be like that.   (Turn to p.182)
But isn't it arrogant for Christians to try to force their
religion on others?   (Turn to p. 111)

1. C. F. G. Masterman, in R. Mudie Smith, *The Religious Life of
London* (London, 1904), 207.
2. James 2:1.6.

3. W. E. H. Lecky, *History of European Morals* (New York, 1955), II, 100–1.
4. Hebrews 1:1.3.
5. Ephesians 2:19–22.
6. Romans 12:4–6.
7. David Watson, *In Search of God* (London, 1979), 97.

QUESTIONS ABOUT CONVERSION

You have said that you agree with the statement

I don't believe in getting 'converted'

This could be your opinion for several reasons. Here are some of the most common reasons people come up with. Tick whichever one(s) may apply to you:

☐ Conversion is just a psychological trick akin to
  brainwashing   (p. 92)
☐ Christians are really no better than other
  people   (p. 95)
☐ You can't be sure you know God—it's all
  wishful thinking   (p. 96)
☐ Sometimes 'conversion' doesn't work. Some are
  the religious sort, some not   (p. 99)
☐ People are no longer religious nowadays:
  they're too sophisticated   (p. 101)
☐ Conversion is caused by fear of hell fire   (p. 104)
☐ The number of people being converted
  nowadays is dropping fast   (p. 106)
☐ Conversion doesn't really change people at a
  deep level   (p. 108)
☐ It is arrogant to force your religion on others   (p. 111)
☐ It doesn't matter what you believe as long as
  you're sincere   (p. 113)

Now turn to the page(s) in this Section on which the answer is given to the statements you have ticked.

◀ Read them, and decide what you think of the answers
   supplied. Then you can go back to the START HERE page
at the beginning of the book, and choose another direction.

▶ Or if you feel you've surveyed the evidence sufficiently
   already, turn straight to Section 9 (YOURSELF)—on p.
187—and follow the instructions there in order to check out
your own position.

Conversion is just a psychological trick akin to brainwashing

How is it that people who firmly believe there is no God will
suddenly change their minds and claim to have had a living
experience of God's reality? How is it that people whose lives
have been selfish and egotistical can suddenly be transformed,
and fling themselves into a career of reckless self-sacrifice and
caring for others? Is it God who brings these changes? Or is it
just something psychological?

New beliefs *can* be implanted by manipulating people's
minds. We know that from the brainwashing practices carried
out by some unscrupulous governments on political prisoners
and prisoners of war. We've seen graphic examples of it in the
rise of mind–bending religious cults over the last twenty years.
But normally such techniques depend on isolation, fear, vivid
suggestions and constant repetition. Does anything like that
happen in Christian conversion?

In 1957, a best-selling paperback claimed that it did. *Battle for
the Mind* was written by Dr. William Sargant, a world-famous
psychologist, who had studied techniques of 'brainwashing' in
many different societies. Sargant was a Methodist, and his
book was endorsed by the Archbishop of Canterbury. But in it
he claimed that famous conversions in the Bible and in
history—St. Paul, the crowd at the Day of Pentecost, John
Wesley—had been secured by unfair mental pressure; and
that Christians were guilty of using the same techniques
today.

What is the truth? Well, there are undeniably psychological
forces at work when people are converted. It's no mere
coincidence that a lot of conversions happen in the mid-
teenage years; that's the age when, psychologically, young

people are making up their minds about what they will believe for the best part of their future lives, and thus they are open to persuasion as they won't ever be again. And sometimes one can see that individual people probably turned to God because of some inbuilt mental inclination, or some deeply-felt psychological need, which conversion helped to resolve. But that doesn't mean that conversion is *just* a psychological phenomenon. There can be more than one level of explanation for anything that happens to us, as we'll see later (p. 111); a conversion can have a psychological explanation *and still*, on another level, be a genuine miraculous outpouring of God's grace into somebody's life.

To make his case sound plausible, Sargant has to leave out a lot of inconvenient details! For example, he points to the Apostle Paul as a clear example of somebody whose mind was tampered with. But he also says, 'A safeguard against conversion is, indeed, a burning and obsessive belief in some creed or way of life.' And nobody had a more 'burning and obsessive belief' than the Apostle Paul before he became a Christian! Yet he did change his mind—despite having what Sargant calls 'a safeguard against conversion' to protect him! It doesn't add up.

The same is true of John Wesley's story. To fit Sargant's theory, Wesley's conversion should have taken place in a crowded, excited meeting; in fact it came about in a quiet discussion group. And when Sargant looks at the story of Pentecost he explains how the three thousand were converted, but not what had happened to the apostles whose strange experience began the whole episode! The facts just don't fit the theory. Psychology can explain some things, but can't explain them away.

Let me give you three other reasons why I firmly believe that conversion really happens, and the Bible is speaking the truth when it says that anyone who becomes a Christian 'is a brand new person inside' (2 Corinthians 5:17, *Living Bible* translation). First, the effects of conversion last, and are big. Brainwashed dupes will often leave their new beliefs as suddenly as they acquired them. But I know men who were murderers who are today as gentle as lambs. I know people who were written off as 'human vegetables' who have passed A–levels and gained good jobs. I know people who were motivated by hatred of the world and themselves, whose personalities have altered completely as they have found in themselves a new love and openness that they never had before. Brainwashing doesn't do this.

Second, conversion to Christianity happens in so many different ways. For some, it's a blinding flash of insight; for others, a long pilgrimage with no awareness of when the final point was reached. For some, it happens in a large meeting; for others, while quietly reading a book. C. S. Lewis became a Christian on the top deck of a bus. For me, it was probably while squashed between four others in the back of a car. For my father, it was in school assembly as a Bible passage was being read by a non-Christian headmaster. You can't make generalizations about psychological tricks when the circumstances are so varied!

Third, conversion happens right across cultures. I know people from nations with a different outlook, education, world view and language from myself, who have had exactly the same experience of Jesus Christ that I have. Visiting their countries and making friends with them just reinforces the impression: their story is no different from mine. We have all met the same person. And he's real.

Do you find this a convincing answer?
☐ YES　　　☐ NO　　　☐ POSSIBLY

If you have further objections to the idea of CONVERSION, read some other parts of this section　　　　　*(pp. 91–114)*

Alternatively you might be asking:

Why is conversion necessary? If God wants us to believe in him, shouldn't he make himself visible?
(Turn to p. 16)
Does God really answer prayer, or is it just a delusion to think so?　　　　　　　　　(Turn to p.162)

Christians are really no better than other people

'Vicar runs off with choir mistress', 'Secret life of Sunday school teacher', 'The preacher with three Rolls Royces'—headlines like that don't improve the image of Christianity, do they? And tabloid newspapers rarely let a month go by without digging up one such story from somewhere. It all confirms the impression many people have: 'These Christians say that Jesus has made them good and holy and whatever, but really under the gloss they're no better than the rest of us. It's all an act.'

So are Christians really better than others?

No, they're not. And the Bible never claims they are. In fact, the first essential for someone who wants to become a Christian is to realize that he's a failure—someone who can't live up to God's standards properly, no matter how he tries. (See p. 185.) Nobody can come to God without making this basic admission first. And then God gets to work on that person's life—forgiving his sins, putting a new moral power inside, implanting new desires to do the right things instead of the wrong.

But that doesn't necessarily make him *better than other people*—just better than he would ever have been without Jesus to help him! You see, we all start from different moral backgrounds. Somebody born in the stockbroker belt of Surrey, with three acres and a pony in the paddock, may find it not too difficult to be a fairly pleasant, genial person, thoughtful and courteous to others. But if you were born in the slums of a big city, with a broken home and poor foster parents, and an education that fitted you only for unemployment benefit, you might understandably have a kingsize chip on your shoulder which it would take years to remove. And if you become a Christian, for a long time you'd probably still be way behind the nice person from the stockbroker belt, as far as personal charm is concerned! So the fair question to ask is not, 'Is person A better than person B?', but, 'Is person A with Christ better than person A without Christ?'

And the answer to this second question, in case after case

after case, has got to be 'Yes'. Both the authors of this book
have been involved for years in presenting the claims of Jesus
Christ to people all over the country, and we've seen the
impact that Christian experience makes on the average human
life. It doesn't turn anyone into an angel, with a faintly
perceptible halo floating six inches above the head! But it *does*
begin a process of change and development which goes on for
the rest of a person's life.

'I am confident of this,' wrote the Apostle Paul, 'that he who
began a good work in you will carry it on to completion until
the day of Christ Jesus.'[1] He was confident because he had
seen it. It works.

⚖️   *Do you find this a convincing answer?*
    ☐ YES   ☐ NO   ☐ POSSIBLY

❗   *If you have further objections to the idea of CONVERSION,
    read some other parts of this section   (pp. 91–114).*

❓   *Alternatively you might be asking:*

    But isn't the church full of hypocrites?
                                            (Turn to p. 84)
    Doesn't it make life tame and uninteresting to become
    a Christian?   (Turn to p. 171)

You can't be sure you know God— it's all wishful thinking

The early Christians were a confident bunch of people. They
didn't just 'think' or 'hope' or 'assume' that they were
Christians. What drove them out to conquer the unfriendly
Roman Empire was their blazing conviction that they *knew*.

And this word 'know' comes up again and again in the New Testament:

> I write these things to you who believe in the name of the Son of God so that you may *know* that you have eternal life.
>   We *know* that in all things God works for the good of those who love him . . .
>   I consider everything a loss compared to the surpassing greatness of *knowing* Christ Jesus my Lord, for whose sake I have lost all things.[2]

How can Christians be so sure? After all, they have never seen Jesus or spoken to him personally. Today's Christians weren't even born when he did his miracles and supposedly rose again. How can you be so certain about something invisible and intangible?

I think there are three things that enable a Christian to be absolutely sure it's not just wishful thinking.

First, *you know by what happens inside you.* If the Bible said, 'Yea verily, when a man shall become a Christian, lo, his nose shall turn green', and it didn't happen, you would immediately be able to say Christianity was untrue. But if it did happen to everyone who professed faith—perhaps there might be something in it!

And the Bible does predict certain results will follow when someone's life is opened up to the transforming power of God's Holy Spirit:

> . . . the fruit of the Spirit is love, joy, peace, patience, kindness, goodness, faithfulness, gentleness and self control . . .[3]

As we have explained already in this section (p. 95), both of us have seen these results slowly begin to appear in the lives of people who become Christians—again and again, too often to be mistaken. We have experienced the same things starting to stir and develop in our own lives as God's power gets to grip with our imperfections. When I see changes in myself that I could never have brought about for myself, I know that a power greater than my own is at work shaping my life.

'Hang on, though,' you might argue. 'How do you know what your subconscious mind can and can't do? Perhaps

you've induced all these changes in yourself by some kind of
self-suggestion or hypnosis. You believe strongly that it's
going to happen to you; and so it does. You're just
subconsciously fulfilling your own prophecy.'

Now that is just possible—though extremely unlikely. But
there's a second reason for being sure. *You know by what
happens outside you.* If God simply affected the 'inside' things,
then certainly it could be just a subjective fantasy. But I find
him at work in 'outside' events too—things I can't imagine, in
the real world. He answers my prayers. He shapes the events
of my life into a meaningful pattern. He brings about
'coincidences' that happen just too often for it to be
coincidence any longer.

I am well aware that it is possible to become too superstitious, and read a deep meaning into every little thing that
happens to you. ('My shoe lace has snapped! What is God
trying to tell me?') But all I can say is that the more sceptical I
try to be, the more the proof presses in on me. To deny that
God is at work in the daily events of my life would be
unrealistic. In fact it would be a lie.

And then there's a third reason for being sure. *You know by
what happens to others.* If I were the only person in the world
who had ever had this strange experience, I might well
seriously consider that I had been deluded. If you got up in the
morning and saw a pig flying past your window, you might
think you had gone mad. But if that morning several hundred
people reported a sighting of an airborne sow, you'd be a little
more confident that your vision had been real! And when
millions of people all over the world have had the same
experience of friendship with God (see p. 106), I can't doubt
any longer that I'm on to something genuine.

I used to spend a lot of my time in Poland. The first time I
went, it was a very strange place. An unpronounceable
language, odd food, weird jokes—a completely different
outlook on life from what I was used to. But I could see in the
lives of Polish Christians, living in a culture totally different
from mine, exactly the same experience of the living Jesus that
I had. And despite the cultural differences there was an
instant bond between us; because we recognized exactly the
same reality in one another.

With all of this going on, it would be hopelessly timid for a

Christian to say, 'I feel I may be in touch with God.' The only word that fits the circumstances is 'I know'. And that's not arrogance. It's a stone-cold sober assessment of the facts.

⚖️ *Do you find this a convincing answer?*
□ YES   □ NO   □ POSSIBLY

❗ *If you have further objections to the idea of CONVERSION, read some other parts of this section*   *(pp. 91–114)*

❓ *Alternatively you might be asking:*

Isn't answered prayer just a delusion?
(Turn to p. 162)
How could I be sure it was all true?   (Turn to p. 180)

Sometimes conversion doesn't work. Some people are the religious sort, some are not

These two statements are both true—on their own. It's when you put them together that you create a false impression. Let me explain!

First, it's true that sometimes 'conversion' doesn't work. Jesus indeed predicted that some people would start to follow him and then be unable to keep it up. And when people jump on the bandwagon of Christianity, without really understanding the kind of commitment which is needed in order to follow Jesus, they may have what looks like a real conversion for a while but in the end they'll drop out and give up.

The famous evangelist D. L. Moody once saw a drunken man weaving his unsteady way down the street. His clothes were filthy and his language was colourful. A bystander said, 'Mr. Moody, do you know who that is? That's one of your converts!' Moody watched the man in silence for a moment.

Finally he said, 'I guess you're right. He certainly isn't one of God's.'

And so it is possible for a 'conversion experience' to be spurious and superficial. But that doesn't take away from the genuineness of the real thing. Jesus promised, 'Whoever has my commands and obeys them, he is the one who loves me . . . My Father will love him, and we will come to him and make our home with him.'[4] And I know from experience that he keeps this promise even today.

Second, it is true that some people are 'the religious sort'. Some people take more naturally to hymnbooks and prayers and stained glass windows and the peculiar smell of churches than others do. But it doesn't mean that 'religious' people are more likely to become Christians. Often, those who become really converted are not 'the religious sort' at all. (Look at Jesus' rough, tough bunch of disciples for a start.) Michael Green explains why this happens:

> Christianity is for non-religious people. It is not going too far to say that if you insist on being religious you will find Christianity hard, almost impossible. You will find it almost impossible to become a Christian, because your 'religion' will get in the way: you will feel that somehow you are better and more pleasing to God than your irreligious neighbour . . . And you will find it almost impossible to be a Christian: because once again your 'religion' will get in the way: you will feel that the Christian life depends on your religious observances, and not on the Lord. You will be inclined to keep a little religious corner in your life for God and not let him have the whole thing.

It is important to remember that one of Jesus' most famous stories is about two men who went into the temple to pray. One was incredibly religious, the other not at all. And the point of the story is that God accepted the non-religious one—whereas the man who was so proud of his religious observances failed completely to make contact with God.

Now do you see why the two statements at the start of this section don't belong together? Sometimes 'conversion' doesn't work—true. But to conclude, 'It's because some people just aren't the religious sort' is completely unrealistic. People drop out of Christianity for many reasons—their commitment wasn't a real one; their enthusiasm was only a momentary flash of interest; they become discouraged by the pressure of other people's disapproval. But people never leave Jesus simply 'because they aren't the religious sort'. Either Christianity is for everyone—or it just isn't true!

Do you find this a convincing answer?
☐ YES   ☐ NO   ☐ POSSIBLY

If you have further objections to the idea of CONVERSION, read some other parts of this section   *(pp. 91–114)*

Alternatively you might be asking:

But can't you worship God without needing to belong to a church?   (Turn to p. 75)
But am I good enough for God to accept me?
(Turn to p. 185)

People are no longer religious nowadays; they're too sophisticated

As we will see (p. 106) there are actually more people becoming Christians today than ever before in the world's history. So in world terms, this statement is just plain wrong. But let's assume you're conceited enough to assume smugly that only Western Europe matters, and the rest of the world is irrelevant. Is it true that in our society today people are no longer religious?

It's certainly true that in most parts of Europe churchgoing has been in decline since the First World War. When you drive through cities and see former churches that have been turned into bingo halls and furniture showrooms; when you watch the congregation come out of an inner city church at the end of a service, and count only five old ladies, a vicar and an organist; and when you inspect a normal residential street on a Sunday morning, and find people washing their cars, sitting in the sun reading their Sunday papers, or heading off to Sainsbury's—it's easy to assume that people today have lost the religious impulse. They just aren't interested.

But churchgoing is only part of the picture. Look at the small ads in the papers, or the guests on TV chat shows. They will show you that there has been a tremendous increase in interest in astrology, clairvoyance, psychic healing, reincarnation, palm reading—people are still looking for answers to basic religious questions about what life means; they're just looking in different places.

Humanist and rationalist groups, who have no religious beliefs, tend to be small gatherings of a few isolated intellectuals. Religious cults of the most dubious and colourful varieties are recruiting successfully all over the world. This is hardly the picture of a society which has abandoned religion.

G. K. Chesterton once commented that when a man stops believing in God, he doesn't believe in nothing—but in anything. And that's what seems to be happening! People are filling up the religious blank in their lives with whatever else they can find which seems to offer the same satisfactions.

For there are some questions which only Christianity can answer satisfactorily, which we need to have answered, and which will never go away and leave us, no matter how long we live. There's the question of guilt. We all know that we do wrong things which need to be forgiven. But how can we have our conscience made clear? Any psychiatrist will tell you that a majority of his patients could be cured straight away if only they could find an answer to that question.

Then there's the question of purpose. We need to know that our life means something and is going somewhere. Says Stanley Kubrick, the film maker:

> If man really sat back and thought about his impending termination, and his terrifying insignificance and aloneness in the cosmos, he would surely go mad, or succumb to a numbing sense of futility. Why, he might ask himself, should he bother to write a great symphony, or strive to make a living, or even to love another, when he is no more

than a momentary microbe on a dust mote whirling through the unimaginable immensity of space?[6]

Finally, there's the question of our death. What happens afterwards? Where do we go? Or is this life all we get? People have struggled with these issues for centuries, and still need to find satisfying answers that will take them through life. Yesterday I visited a man in hospital who is dying of cancer. He has been a Christian for many years, and although now he is weak, most of the time only semi-conscious, and pitifully wasted, his firm sense of the reality and love of Jesus Christ is giving him a confidence in the face of death which the nursing staff readily admit they're not used to seeing. Has he discovered an answer which people in our society desperately need to find?

In fact, some research done at Nottingham University has shown that people today are just as likely as ever to have a sense of the infinite, a perception that there's someone there who is bigger than they are. They may not be church-goers, but a surprising number of modern people claim to have felt the reality of God. Summing up the research, zoologist David Hay calls it 'an extraordinary phenomenon. Why should so many people have religious experience to report? I doubt very much that religion is about to die out. The awareness out of which it grows is too widespread for that.'[7]

But such a glimmering awareness of God, important as it is, is a long way from the calm confidence and firm assurance of my dying friend. It's not enough to have an experience which remains mysterious and unintelligible because you have no key to understanding it. The satisfaction arrives only when a human being meets his Creator for the first time and knows that he is forgiven, accepted, given a new life. And nobody, even in modern Western Europe, is too sophisticated to need such an encounter.

Do you find this a convincing answer?
☐ YES ☐ NO ☐ POSSIBLY

If you have further objections to the idea of CONVERSION, read some other parts of this section (pp. 91–114)

Alternatively you might be asking:

But what the church does is boring and outdated—
isn't it?   (Turn to p. 88)

Conversion is caused by fear of hell fire

This objection is often raised by people who just can't see why
anyone in his senses would want to accept all the difficulties
involved in being a Christian. What do you get out of it? And
so they conclude: the explanation must be that people are
terrified into it. Scared by the fear of hell fire.

There are actually lots of good reasons for becoming a
Christian, and if you need an answer to the question 'What do
you get out of it?' you should really be reading p. 149. But it's
undeniably true that warning people about judgment and hell
was part of the original Christian message. (If you want to
know more about this, go to p. 127.) And one of the largest
church revivals in history began with a sermon by an
American preacher entitled 'Sinners in the Hands of an Angry
God'.

Reading that title, many people imagine that the preacher
—Jonathan Edwards—must have brought his audience to
fever pitch by dramatic oratory, inflamed their imaginations by
vivid techniques, and worked on mass hysteria to achieve a
conditioning effect. But if the historical records are true,
Edwards (who was one of America's greatest intellectuals
anyway) simply read his sermons in a high-pitched, thin,
unemotional voice, by the light of a candle. The effects which
followed were nothing to do with unscrupulous psychological
manipulation.

The same thing is true about the early Christian preachers.
Hell was part of their message, but hardly the main part. And
they didn't dwell on it to terrify their hearers into submission.
They simply stated clearly the choice that men and women
had to make, and left it at that.

Scaring people can actually be counter-productive. When I
was eleven I was so terrified by a sermon on the Second

Coming of Jesus Christ that I decided I wanted to be a Christian. But it was pure fright, not real commitment. Nothing changed in my young life, and it wasn't for another few years that I found a genuine relationship with God.

But supposing someone does become a Christian largely because he is worried about the prospect of facing God's condemnation. What's so wrong about that? If judgement is real, and needs to be avoided, he is actually making a thoroughly rational move. And if you object, 'But that's a selfish reason for becoming a Christian'—well, most reasons are.

I suppose the only truly pure reason for accepting Christ would be sheer gratitude for Jesus' act of self-sacrifice in dying on the cross. But very few people have such pure motives, because people are basically selfish. We want what we can get for ourselves. It's *after* we become Christians that God starts taking the selfishness away—not before!

And so we may come to God for a whole variety of selfish motives—our lives are empty, and we feel he can offer us fulfilment; our marriage problems have made us desperate, and we have nowhere else to turn; we are anxious to escape God's judgement, and here is an escape route. It doesn't matter what the motive may be. If we are genuinely willing to be forgiven and made new, God will keep his promise and begin to turn us into better, selfless people.

It's a bit like getting married. When a man starts to be attracted to a woman, he may just notice how good looking she is. There may be no more to it than that; his ego may just be gratified by the fact that he has such a beautiful creature sitting in the passenger seat of his sports car. But if a real relationship is to form,eventually he will begin noticing and liking other things about her too. And then he will start to love her for herself—not just for superficial, selfish reasons.

The point is not the original motive but the end result. Don't write off other people's conversions because you feel the motive was unworthy. And don't miss out on Jesus Christ yourself because this particular motive has no appeal to you!

Do you find this a convincing answer?
☐ YES ☐ NO ☐ POSSIBLY

If you have further objections to the idea of CONVERSION, read some other parts of this section   *(pp. 91–114)*

Alternatively you might be asking:

Who wants eternal life, anyway—surely it must be boring?   (Turn to p. 135)
Isn't religion just a distraction when we have bigger problems to solve?   (Turn to p. 157)

The number of people being converted nowadays is dropping fast

This is a common mistake that people make. Until the 1970s, it was more or less assumed that the church was shrinking worldwide—that fewer and fewer people were becoming Christians. Conversion was a thing of the past.

But then research agencies started counting. And some interesting things were discovered. It was found out, for example, that people are becoming Christians nowadays at a faster rate than ever before in world history. The total number of Christians of all sorts increased from 558 million in the year 1900 to 1433 million by 1980. In the Third World the difference was even more striking—83 million at the start of the 20th century had become 634 million eighty years later. There are countries where three times as many people are becoming Christians as are being born!

The Bible is available, in whole or in part, in languages spoken by 97% of the world's population. Not surprisingly, this meant that in 1980 eight times as many Bibles and New Testaments were sold as in 1900. The total figure was a staggering 36 million Bibles and 57 million New Testaments. The Bible is still the world's undisputed best-seller.

In 1980, every Sunday, 2,000 churches opened their doors that just hadn't been there the Sunday before. Every minute, fifty-eight new people somewhere around the world became

Christians. And 8,000 of the world's cultures have been penetrated to some degree by the Christian faith. Today there are Christians and organized churches in practically every country on earth.

Is this something that is just happening in ignorant, undeveloped areas of the world? Hardly (and it's worth remembering anyway that 'undeveloped' doesn't necessarily mean 'ignorant'!). In sophisticated societies such as Japan and the USA, the church is growing massively. In America 65% of the population is said to attend a place of worship on Sunday. In Japan, which was for so long an unresponsive mission field for Western churches to send missionaries to, there are now home-grown missionary societies sending out Japanese Christians to spread the Christian message in other continents!

Now this does not mean that the Christian church has completed her job. There are a lot of non-Christians left! The world's population has been rocketing, too, and so the Christian percentage of the world has remained more or less the same since 1900. But there are signs that by the turn of the century—especially in Africa and South America—the Christian faith will be doing better than ever before.

Also, it's possible that these figures include many people who may write down 'Christian' when asked to state their religion on a form, but who know very little about the real friendship of Jesus Christ. For all that, it's staggering that two thousand years after Jesus' death in shame and disgrace, one-third of the world claims to follow him, and one-tenth claims a personal relationship with him.

It almost makes you think the whole story could possibly be true. Doesn't it?

Do you find this a convincing answer?
☐ YES   ☐ NO   ☐ POSSIBLY

If you have further objections to the idea of CONVERSION, read some other parts of this section   *(pp. 91–114)*

Alternatively you might be asking:

That's all very well, but why are there so many splits
and divisions in the church?   (Turn to p. 80)
Isn't the church just a device used by the rich to
oppress the poor?   (Turn to p. 69)

Conversion doesn't really change people at a deep level

If this is what you think, the chances are you've met someone
who tried Christianity for a while and then gave up. Or
somebody who claims to be a Christian, but is actually quite an
obvious hypocrite.

Well, don't judge by individual cases. Get to know some
more Christians, watch them closely, and see if they 'ring
true'. I'm sure you'll be convinced after a while that—whether
Christianity is true or not—it really does bring about a deep
and permanent change.

And be careful that you aren't looking for the wrong kinds
of changes! The Bible doesn't promise a change in a person's
circumstances, for example. Never believe books with titles
like *How I trusted the Lord and tripled my profits*—implying that
anyone who becomes a Christian will do well financially. The
facts are that 62% of the world church lives in comparative
poverty (and the inequalities between Christians of different
races are one of the biggest problems the church must start to
sort out). This is a world in which innocent people suffer (see
p. 151) and God doesn't guarantee you a villa by the
Mediterranean as a fringe benefit when you give him your life.

Nor does the Bible promise to change our emotions. Human
feelings constantly fluctuate; one day we'll be ecstatically
happy, the next day depressed, and you never know what's
coming next. Your emotions can be influenced by the weather,
how tired you are, whether the little red-headed girl is paying

any attention to you, even occasional irrational bursts of wild jubilation or unexpected misery. And it would be unnatural for God to take your very human, helter-skelter emotional pattern and fix it artificially, so that you sat permanently on Cloud Nine with a rigid plastic grin on your face.

There are good times and bad times in Christian living. There's a deep, settled joy at the back of all your circumstances, and it gives you the resilience to go on; but fluttery feelIngs of happiness aren't what God promises.

So it is wrong to expect (as so many people do!) that when you become a Christian, a strange and holy feeling will magically descend upon your tummy and make you feel good. Some people do feel a tremendous emotional release when they become Christians; others feel nothing at all; and in either case, they'll probably feel quite different within twenty-four hours, so there's no point in relying upon how you do or don't feel.

Third, God doesn't change our will by taking away all our responsibility to make moral choices for ourselves. ᵕome people feel that when you become a Christian, God should programme your brain so that you automatically live in a holy and upright way, completely immune from temptation and desire. Wrong. God doesn't want zombies, but people who freely choose to love him and serve him with all they've got. He does give us a new power to help us combat evil and live for right, but he doesn't make it irresistible. If you want to apply the Holy Spirit's power to your temptations and sins, you have to choose to do so.

What does a real conversion change, then? All sorts of things. It changes a person's whole outlook on life, for a start. As you grow used to the presence of Jesus in your life, you begin to see things through his eyes, and make his priorities yours. You catch yourself reacting to situations in ways you'd never have dreamed of, a few months before. Conversion changes your approach to life; knowing Jesus' love as a daily reality increases your confidence in yourself as a person, your ability to relate to others, your desire to do whatever you can to help them rather than simply living for yourself. And your moral reactions change, as you learn to allow the Holy Spirit's power to deal with area after area in your life where some sweeping clean and sorting out is required. You start to catch glimpses of the calmness and peace which trusting Jesus can bring into your life; and suddenly other people are remarking on the difference in you. It's a bit like coming into a whole new world. Except that, when you get there, it feels as if you've come home to where you belong for the first time in your existence.

If you know some Christians who aren't a good advertisement for all this, as we suggested above, bear three things in mind. First, as we've seen (p. 95), everybody starts from a different point, so remember that the Holy Spirit has a little more work to do on some of us! Second, remember that the Bible teaches that the change in us will never be complete until we reach heaven; don't expect perfection from Christians— just progress. And, third, remember that even Christians can sometimes stop co-operating with the Holy Spirit, which means that their Christian life becomes temporarily unreal. 2 Peter 1:5–11 speaks very honestly about this problem.

But wouldn't it be tragic if you let the imperfections of other people deter you from having the greatest, most exciting experience in the world?

Do you find this a convincing answer?
☐ YES   ☐ NO   ☐ POSSIBLY

If you have further objections to the idea of CONVERSION, read some other parts of this section   *(pp. 91–114)*

Alternatively you might be asking:

Aren't Christians obsessed with saving their own souls at the expense of the world?   (Turn to p. 173)
But haven't Christians been starting wars for centuries?   (Turn to p. 81)

It is arrogant to force your religion on others

Agreed. To force people to accept Christ at the point of a sword, or through some kind of blackmail, is quite unacceptable. Usually, too, it doesn't work; the converts will return to their former beliefs as soon as your back is turned. And serve you right.

It is right, however, to reason with other people and to try to persuade them. As long as you are not coercing them by some kind of unfair emotional pressure, it isn't wrong to use every argument at your disposal to help people see the exciting potential of what you have found in Jesus, and convince them that they need to share it too. Not to do this wouldn't be fair to them. If you really believe that you have found in Jesus Christ the one and only solution to the gravest problems confronting the human race, you'd have to be truly selfish not to want to broadcast the news as widely as ever you could.

This, of course, is assuming that you believe you have something vital to share. If you believe that all religions say one and the same thing (and we've dealt with that idea on p. 73), you will naturally feel diffident about touting to the world your favourite version of what everybody's already got anyway. Dr. Sarvepalli Radhakrishnan, the great Hindu scholar, never really understood Christianity, which, he complained, was riddled with 'absolute dogmatism', 'intolerance' and 'exclusiveness'. And this was because he saw all religions as leading in the same direction:

> Rites, ceremonies, systems and dogmas . . . are not to be mistaken for absolute truth. They are used to communicate the shadow of what has been realized . . . The signpost is not the destination.[8]

However, Jesus insisted that 'no-one comes to the Father except through me'. That he had something to offer the world which was absolutely unique and unpredecented, and that anyone who deliberately turned his back on Jesus Christ would never find the true light of life. If this is true, it would be grossly unfair not to tell the whole world about it. And to do so is not arrogant, because Christians are not claiming to be anyone special; they didn't find out about Jesus through their own superior spirituality, or their incredibly penetrating brain; they have simply stumbled on a secret which belongs to all the people, and they are passing it on because they daren't do otherwise.

Now it is true that sometimes Christians have been insensitive and overbearing in the way they have done this. But do remember that it's hard to be 'laid back' when you believe you are conveying a life-or-death message! And it's true some Christians have been proud and pompous in the way they've shared their faith. But often that is simply a cover for lack of confidence and fear of rejection.

Suppose you are a doctor who knows the only cure for a particular deadly disease. And one day you come across someone who is dying of the disease—but who could be saved if you told him about the cure. Would you really think, 'No, it's arrogant to force my cure on other people', and leave him to die? Or would you do your utmost to persuade the dying man to take the medicine?

Now suppose you're the patient. Would you really refuse to take the cure just because you couldn't stand the doctor who offered it to you?

Don't make the same mistake with Christianity!

Do you find this a convincing answer?
☐ YES   ☐ NO   ☐ POSSIBLY

If you have further objections to the idea of CONVERSION, read some other parts of this section   *(pp. 91–114)*

Alternatively you might be asking:

Can't I worship God without belonging to a church?
(Turn to p. 75)
Surely the Bible can be read in many different ways? Who's to say that any one interpretation is correct?
(Turn to p. 53)

It doesn't matter what you believe as long as you're sincere

I believe that Adolf Hitler was God. Jews should be murdered. Gypsies should be disembowelled publicly and their remains fed to little children. I believe that the London Underground is a tool of the Antichrist, and trains must be set on fire wherever possible. I believe it is morally justifiable to explode a bomb in the middle of a football crowd. I believe that grasshoppers are a superior form of life who must be invited to rule this planet . . .

Would you accept all those statements as valid beliefs? Of course not. If I came out with too many statements like that, you'd have me locked up. Yet I could be perfectly sincere in believing them!

And if it doesn't matter what you believe as long as you're sincere, these beliefs and ideas are just as worthy and important as yours!

Do you see the point? It's possible for someone to be sincere and wrong. All the sincerity in the world won't save you from the results of your own errors. If you get on a train heading for Derby sincerely believing it's going to Plymouth, your sincerity won't be enough to turn the train round and make it go in the direction you want. You will just have to admit your mistake and get off the wrong train.

In the same way, religious believers of all sorts can be perfectly sincere in all they profess. They may be absolutely convinced that what they believe is incontrovertibly true. But if they've got it wrong, their sincerity will be of no use. They will have to admit their mistake and change trains!

It's a good thing, really, that God doesn't actually judge us on our sincerity. For human beings are often very insincere. We say one thing, and do another. We claim to stand for certain principles, and then when the pressure is on we compromise. I know how much basic dishonesty there is in me, and I would guess that you're not much different. If God looked for total sincerity, which of us would stand a chance?

But God's standard of judgement is different. God wants to know how we have responded to the truth when it has been presented to us. And if what we have said so far in this book is true, Jesus Christ is the truth in a unique way. He can do for you what 'sincerity' never could. He can change your whole life . . .

Of course it matters what you believe; it matters desperately. Make sure you choose correctly, because if you don't bother to do so, all the sincerity you can muster will never substitute for what you will be depriving yourself of.

Do you find this a convincing answer?
☐ YES   ☐ NO   ☐ POSSIBLY

If you have further objections to the idea of CONVERSION, read some other parts of this section (pp. 91–114). If you have read this whole section, go back to the START HERE page (p. 1) and choose another direction.

Alternatively you might be asking:

But isn't it arrogant to believe human life has any value in a meaningless universe?   (Turn to p. 155)
How can God condemn those who have not heard the Christian message?   (Turn to p. 129)

1. Philippians 1:6.
2. 1 John 5:13; Romans 8:28; Philippians 3:8.
3. Galatians 5:22–3.
4. John 14:21–3.
5. E. M. B. Green, *You Must Be Joking!* (London, 1976), 19–20.
6. From 'The Playboy Interview', in Jerome Agel, ed., *The Making of Kubrick's 2001* (New York, 1970), 352–3.
7. David Hay, *Exploring Inner Space* (Harmondsworth, 1982), 212.
8. S. Radhakrishnan, *East and West, the End of their Separation* (New York, 1954); quoted by Stephen Neill, *Crises of Belief* (London, 1984), 108.

QUESTIONS ABOUT LIFE AND DEATH

You have said that you agree with the statement

I find the Christian view of Life, Death, Heaven and Hell unsatisfactory

This could be your opinion for several reasons. Here are some of the most common reasons people come up with. Tick whichever one(s) may apply to you.

☐ Human beings are just sophisticated machines (p. 116)
☐ When you're dead you rot (p. 118)
☐ Contacts with the dead have disproved
Christianity (p. 121)
☐ We come back for life after life (p. 124)
☐ A God of love could not let people go to hell (p. 127)
☐ How can God condemn those who have never
heard the Christian message? (p. 129)
☐ Now that we can create life artificially, we have
no need of God (p. 131)
☐ Eternal life would be boring (p. 135)
☐ People have died and returned to life, but have
never seen a heaven or hell (p. 136)
☐ Human beings cannot be special because there
must be millions of races like ourselves in our
galaxy (p. 139)

Now turn to the page(s) in this Section on which the answer is given to the statements you have ticked.

◀ Read them, and decide what you think of the answers
supplied. Then you can go back to the START HERE page
at the beginning of the book, and choose another direction.

➧ Or if you feel you've surveyed the evidence sufficiently
   already, turn straight to Section 9 (YOURSELF)—on p.
187—and follow the instructions there in order to check out
your own position.

Human beings are just sophisticated machines

Did you know that if your brain cells were people, there would
be enough of them to populate twenty-five planets the size of
earth? That inside your body you have sixty thousand miles of
inner tubing? That the number of interconnections in just one
human brain rivals the number of all the stars and galaxies in
the universe?

Human beings are sophisticated machines—nobody could
question that. But does that mean we're nothing more? Are we
just sophisticated machines?

The kind of argument which lies behind such a claim runs
something like this. 'We can now describe pretty accurately
exactly why people do the things they do. People can be
conditioned and manipulated by advertisers, brainwashers,
genetic architects. Soon we will know all there is to know
about human motivation. Human beings aren't free, responsible creatures made in God's image; they're robots respond-
ing to certain stimuli. You don't need to drag in God to explain
human behaviour—we have found other, better answers.'

Sounds plausible? Well, perhaps. But first consider a few
things.

For one, is 'explaining' the same thing as 'explaining away'?
Or can there be more than one level of explanation involved in
a full description? For example, if I walk across the room, you
could explain what I am doing in terms of displacement of
molecules, or the co-ordination of certain muscles, and give a
full physical, chemical and physiological account of my
behaviour. But you still wouldn't have answered the question,
'Why has this man chosen to take a walk across the room?'
Because the language of purposes and reasons and motives is

a different level of explanation. Just as real—and just as important.

D. R. Hofstadter illustrated the point like this:

> Say you are having a hard time making up your mind whether to order a cheeseburger or a pineappleburger. Does this imply that your neurons are also balking, having difficulty decoding whether or not to fire? Of course not. Your hamburger confusion is a high-level state which fully depends on the efficient firing of thousands of neurons in very organized ways.[1]

The kind of description which uses words like 'neuron' and 'synapse' is a different kind from the sort which talks about 'choices' and 'indecisiveness'. Yet both levels are absolutely real. So what?

Well, perhaps this suggests that a description of humans as 'sophisticated machines' might make sense on a lot of different levels—but on other levels might leave out something absolutely crucial. Like meaning, purpose, happiness, fulfilment. Mere scientific description can impart very little content to questions like this. Questions such as: 'What are humans for?'

If you came downstairs one morning, opened the living room door, and found a gleaming silver machine standing on the carpet—lights glowing, cogs turning, ticking noises coming from its motors—your first question would be, 'What's that thing for?' And you wouldn't feel you had received a complete answer if the rest of your family simply replied, 'Oh, it isn't for anything, really. It's just a machine.' You'd expect a sophisticated machine to have a purpose for its existence. Wouldn't it seem fair to expect the same of human beings?

To say we are 'just a machine' is to fall into a philosophical error known as 'ontological reductionism' (or, less politely, 'nothing-buttery'!). To say that a signpost is 'nothing but' a piece of wood held together by iron shafts and daubed with marks in pigment isn't a good enough explanation. You need to think as well about what it says. And if the notice reads, 'DANGER—Blasting in Progress', you neglect that extra level of significance at great peril!

Are there things about us which suggest the need of an extra level of explanation—one which includes God and purpose?

There are plenty. Take the human hunger for meaning, for a start. Human beings have agonized for centuries over the significance of human life; and our optimism and creativity as a race depend on the belief that there is some significance and point in human existence. Take the life of Jesus, which demonstrated something never seen before in the world's history—and leaves us with questions which are absolutely insoluble unless there is a God and Jesus really came from him. Take the existence of religion in every known culture in the world. Human beings instinctively believe in something greater than themselves, claim in large numbers to have had contact with it (see p. 103), and desperately need help in understanding it more fully.

These are just pointers; none of them, by themselves, prove the existence of the 'God' level of explanation. But it does suggest that at least you have to take it seriously. And that if you write humans off as 'just sophisticated machines', you might be ignoring the most crucial facts of all about human beings—the facts which give us any meaning and purpose at all.

⚖️   *Do you find this a convincing answer?*
      ☐ YES   ☐ NO   ☐ POSSIBLY

❗   *If you have further objections to the Christian view of LIFE AND DEATH, read some other parts of this section*
                                          (pp. 115–141)

❓   *Alternatively you may be asking:*
But doesn't the idea of evolution do away with the need for God? (Turn to p. 9)

When you're dead, you rot

When Alexei Kosygin was premier of the Soviet Union, his wife died. She was buried in solemn state, with Kosygin as chief mourner, and the service was televised. Viewers all over the world saw a strange thing happen as the coffin finally disappeared from sight. Kosygin leaned forward and placed on top of it an evergreen branch—the Russian symbol of everlasting life.

What an odd thing for the leader of the world's foremost materialist, atheist state to do. And of course for Kosygin it was probably just a romantic, hopeless gesture; he didn't really believe in everlasting life; he just didn't want to accept that the person he loved had come to an abrupt and awful termination. That there was nothing left behind of a life he had held precious.

But Kosygin's gesture does emphasize something important. Human beings have always tended to believe in life after death, and have found it hard to throw the idea away. In just about every culture known to man, there are signs of a belief in survival beyond the tomb; there are even traces, it seems, in Neanderthal remains of sixty thousand years ago.

'Oh, come on,' you might say. 'It's all wishful thinking. Primitive savages didn't know half as much as we know today about death. It was easy for them to believe in an after life . . .'

Really? You could argue that the opposite was true. We have turned our backs on death to such an extent that we rarely meet it any more. Centuries ago, the lower life expectancy, the merciless plagues for which cures were unknown, and the absence of hospitals to which the sick could be discreetly whisked off, meant that people were surrounded constantly by the agonizing, implacable presence of death. People knew that bodies rotted. There were no sanitized crematoria to reduce the problem to a neat pile of ashes, no funeral beauticians to rouge the cheeks of corpses and make them look good for their final journey. The questions posed by death were more immediate, more harsh, than ever they are for us. And still people believed in an after life.

The question you have to ask is: was it all just a wistful fairy story—a way of dealing with the problem by denying its importance? Or are there good grounds for believing that something lies beyond the grave?

The first thing to be said is that there is no reason why survival after death should not be possible. A human being is more than just his body. The personality, the individual aspect which makes us unique, is more than just a function of our physiology. The essential ingredient of the human mind is not the 'hardware'—the material the brain is made of—but the 'software'—the way that material organizes itself, the 'programme' the computer runs. 'The software description of the mind does not logically require neurons,' states J. A. Fodor in *Scientific American*; '. . . it allows for the existence of disembodied minds . . . Functionalism does not rule out the possibility, however remote it may be, of . . . ethereal systems having mental states and processes.'[2]

And there is a great deal of data which suggests that 'disembodied minds' do actually exist, and sometimes communicate with us. Dr. John Beloff is a humanist, and has no belief in a God at all; but in 1965 he wrote that the evidence points to a 'dualistic world where mind or spirit has an existence separate from the world of material things'. He said that he and his fellow unbelievers 'cannot afford to close our minds . . . to the possibility of some kind of survival'.[3] The data is complicated, and we shouldn't rush to conclusions about it (as you will see in the next few pages)—but nonetheless it is there, and it would be dishonest simply to ignore it.

Even more convincing, for a Christian, is the evidence for Jesus' resurrection (see p. 33). There is good evidence that one man has actually conquered death and returned to life. And if Christians are correct in their claim that this person can be known and communicated with today, then their experience of him is absolute proof that life after death happens.

Let's face it, human beings are the most intricate, complex, miraculous product of nature that we know. Does it make sense to believe that nature would produce her greatest masterpiece, allow it to flourish for a few brief years, and then suddenly wipe it all out? Or is it more logical to conclude that anything as fully developed and complicated as ourselves is likely to have a purpose and significance beyond this limited existence?

You can work out your opinion about that for yourself. But one thing isn't just a matter of opinion. If Jesus Christ is genuinely, undeniably, demonstrably, unmistakably alive and kicking, then life after death takes place. Prove Jesus is real—and you've proved survival.

⚖️ *Do you find this a convincing answer?*
☐ YES   ☐ NO   ☐ POSSIBLY

❗ *If you have further objections to the Christian view of LIFE AND DEATH, read some other parts of this section*
(pp. 115–141)

❓ *Alternatively you may be asking:*

Is there any evidence that Jesus rose from the dead?
(Turn to p. 33)
Didn't the whole idea of a God arise from primitive superstitions?
(Turn to p. 15)

Contacts with the dead have disproved Christianity

When the son of Bishop James Pike committed suicide in 1966, his father went to a Spiritualist medium in the hope that she could make contact with Jim Jr. in the world beyond the grave. Sure enough, the dead boy began communicating, and some of the messages he brought were about religion. Here is a sample:

'They talk about Jesus as a mystic, a seer, yes, a seer. I haven't met him. Oh, but Dad, they don't talk about him as a Saviour. As an example, you see? Don't you ever believe that God can be personalized. He is the Central Force, and you all give your quota toward it.'

Now if you have read this book carefully enough, you will notice straight away that these ideas from beyond the grave are very different from the traditional claims about God and Jesus. And this is usual in this kind of communication.

Christian ideas about reality aren't supported by what the dead tell us. So doesn't this throw doubt on Christianity?

But wait a minute. Is it really the dead who are passing on this information?

'It has to be,' many people would reply. 'There are mediums who can give you messages from your loved ones which contain details the medium herself couldn't possibly have known. There are thousands of cases of successful communication. It has to be real.'

Well, if so, there are some puzzling facts to be explained. First, why do so many of the spirit messages conflict with one another? For example: some spirits have passed on the information that after death we all eventually return to earth for another lifetime here with a different identity. Other spirits deny this possibility; and as a result Spiritualists are divided about what to believe. Obviously, *some* of these spirits at least have got to be lying!

Again, most communicators—like Jim Pike Jr.—teach that Jesus is not the Son of God at all. But just a few others have claimed that he is! And that has caused a major split in world Spiritualism—between the 'Christian Spiritualists' (who have a certain allegiance to Jesus, although they're certainly not Christians) and the majority (who have no particular allegiance to Jesus).

It's worrying, too, that so many communications are so trivial. The messages are vague, repetitive and inconsequential. We have had almost a century and a half of organized Spiritualism now, and we haven't yet found out anything much worth knowing about the next world. You would think that voyagers in the world of the dead, who have uncovered the secrets we all long to know about, would have a little more to report.

Then again there are lies and deception. One of the greatest of early mediums, Eusapia Palladino, once said to an investigator who was testing her, 'Watch me or I'll cheat; John King makes me cheat' ('John King' being the spirit guide who was the source of her communications). After studying spirit communications, G. K. Chesterton commented, 'The only thing I will say with complete confidence, about that mystic and invisible power, is that it tells lies.'

What are we to make of it all?

Obviously, that it would be foolish to believe naively in the truth of every message that claimed to come from the dead. The Bible seems to claim that trying to contact the dead at all is a silly and dangerous exercise (read Isaiah ch. 8, for instance), and there are at least two reasons why that should be true.

First, there is plenty of evidence to show that sometimes a medium is not relaying a message from the dead at all, but is by some sort of telepathy picking up memories and ideas from the brain of the person she is trying to help, and then feeding those things back in the form of a message. This explains why sometimes the medium seems to have learned things she couldn't possibly have found out by research; she has actually picked them up from tuning in unconsciously to your own brain!

For example, one evening while Mrs. W. H. Salter was in a seance, she received a message which seemed to come from her dead father, Professor A. W. Verrall, recounting a story about once having worn two pairs of trousers simultaneously. Could it be a pure coincidence that Mrs. Salter had heard the same story told about someone else, just the evening before? Or was it her memory of the story which the medium had picked up and transformed into a 'communication'?

Second, the Bible warns that there are beings in the universe who are disembodied, but able to communicate with humans, and that they are endlessly deceptive and destructive. It's possible that their activity lies behind some of the 'communications' which fascinate people. I have no space to make a case for this here, but let me note two points: first, some (non-Christian!) parapsychologists are starting to believe in the existence of evil personal forces in some of the phenomena they are studying; second, in the history of those who have delved deeply into this subject there is a ghastly trail littered with broken marriages, suicides, alcoholism, breakdowns, sexual perversion . . .

So why should you believe communications of such dubious and possibly dangerous origin? But if on the other hand someone came back from the dead, and was able to prove his reality to you not by spooky messages or party tricks such as levitating tables, but by being there quietly and consistently in your life day by day, shaping it, teaching you new lessons all the time, answering your prayers and satisfying your life—he would be a little more dependable as a source of information, wouldn't he?

But that doesn't happen. Does it?

Do you find this a convincing answer?
☐ YES   ☐ NO   ☐ POSSIBLY

!

If you have further objections to the Christian view of LIFE AND DEATH, read some other parts of this section
(pp.115–141)

?

Alternatively you may be asking:

If Christianity is true why doesn't God do miracles today?   (Turn to p. 178)
Isn't it possible that Jesus was just a teacher who never claimed to be God?   (Turn to p. 35)

We come back for life after life

Arnall Bloxham is a hypnotherapist in Cardiff. He has used his skills to help people with a wide variety of medical and psychological problems. But he has also—or so he claims— used hynosis to help people remember details of past lives they have lived already on this planet, in another century, with a different identity. Over twenty years, he has tape-recorded more than four hundred examples of 'hypnotic regression'.

Do people live more than once?

Bloxham says, 'I am actually a Christian, and of course a Christian doesn't need to believe anything particularly . . . You can believe anything you like. And so I believe in reincarnation.'

But wait a minute! The early Christians seem to have had very decided views about what you could and couldn't believe. Paul wrote to Timothy, for instance, 'In later times some will abandon the faith and follow deceiving spirits and things taught by demons . . . Have nothing to do with godless myths and old wives' tales . . . Watch your life and doctrine closely.' Clearly, you couldn't just believe *anything* and call yourself a Christian.

And one of the things the early Christians very definitely believed is summed up in Hebrews 9:27. 'Man is destined to die once, and after that to face judgement.' No second chances; no successive incarnations. And so if reincarnation is true, Christianity is false.

So what is the state of the evidence?

There are two main reasons why reincarnation is an increasingly popular belief in Britain today. One is *deja vu*; the other is hypnotic regression. Many people think that these two phenomena prove indisputably that we have lived before.

Deja vu is the sense that we sometimes get, when we go to an unfamiliar place, of somehow having been there before. Everything seems uncannily familiar. Yet we know that in this lifetime we have never previously visited this spot. Could it be that we knew the place in a former existence?

Unfortunately, *deja vu* is fairly easily explained. It's basically a 'disrhythmic functioning' (to quote the *Encyclopaedia Britannica*) of the twin lobes of the brain. It's a simple mental illusion which means very little; and it is much more common in some kinds of people than others—epileptics, for example, and those who have had brain surgery, or are experiencing serious deprivation of food. The way in which it occurs tends to support the claim that it's just a delusive mental phenomenon.

Hypnotic regression at first sight looks very impressive. Subjects give detailed information about the circumstances of their previous lives, and a lot of it turns out to be very plausible indeed. And yet the people concerned may never even have read a book about the historical period which they are 'remembering'. Where is all this information coming from, if not from sunken memories of previous lives?

In some cases, the answer may be: imagination. That was the case with the earliest and most famous case of hypnotic regression, in which an American society lady turned into 'Bridey Murphy', an Irish peasant girl of the century before. The story seemed unbelievably accurate—until some facts were discovered about the lady's childhood which showed that her subconscious mind was simply jumbling together reminiscences of neighbours, stories she had been told, and events of her own past.

But that can't account for everything. Is there another possible source of information?

We have already noticed (p. 123) that mediums who go into trance seem able to 'pick the lock' of somebody else's subconscious mind and memories, and lift information which can be turned into a 'message'. There is just a little evidence to suggest that this may even happen with the mind and memories of someone who has died. It's possible, at least, that people who are reressed hypnotically go into a state in which they are able to perform the same feat, and feed on the memories of someone else as if they were their own. You can't prove that this happens; but it seems just as possible as the 'previous lives' theory, and fits many cases much better.

So there can be other explanations, besides previous existences, for the phenomena which are sometimes claimed to prove reincarnation. And there are lots of philosophical questions a believer in reincarnation has to resolve. If we all come back for repeated lives, why is the population of the world growing so quickly? Why do so many claimants turn out to have been Queen Victoria or Cleopatra? In what sense does the same person return, if 'he' is coming back with a completely different identity? Which of his 'selves' is he? And if you say, 'None of them—there's a kind of Super-self controlling them all', why is he never conscious of the existence of this 'Super-self', and how can you prove it exists?

Maybe Paul was right to advise Timothy to stick to the doctrine he'd already been taught?

Do you find this a convincing answer?
☐ YES   ☐ NO   ☐ POSSIBLY

If you have further objections to the Christian view of LIFE AND DEATH, read some other parts of this section
(pp. 115–141)

Alternatively you may be asking:

But your view is based on the Bible; can't the Bible be
interpreted in many different ways?   (Turn to p. 53)
Isn't it just that Christians are obsessed with the need
to save their souls?   (Turn to p. 173)

A God of love could not let people go to Hell

I can understand this objection. It seems a bit incongruous,
doesn't it, when you look at all those mediaeval pictures of
demons with pitchforks herding terrified lost souls down into
the flames, so that they can burn in torment for ever and
ever—and then you reflect that Christianity is supposed to be
about a God of love. It doesn't seem to fit.

But then when you read the Bible you find that no-one in the
New Testament talked about hell more than Jesus did. It
seems to have been a non-detachable part of his message. So
was he wrong? And if he was wrong, is there anything left of
Christianity?

I think that if you're going to sort this question out you need
to look closely at the three key words in the statement above:
'God', 'love' and 'hell'. Let's do that.

First of all, what kind of 'God' does the Bible talk about? As
we've seen in this book already, a God who is a person—not a
Celestial Examining Board who will one day impassively grade
each of us as 'Passed' or 'Failed—please destroy'. And so what
God wants from us, more than anything else, is not a
performance—a spotlessly pure moral life with no grey bits
whatsoever—but a personal relationship. He doesn't insist
that we live up to impossible ideals and kill ourselves trying to
be good before he will admit us to his air-conditioned palace in
the sky. He does invite us to turn from the mess we have made
of our lives, accept his forgiveness, and begin on a lifetime of
friendship and trust in his company. The offer is open and free
if only we will accept it. But you can't force people to be
friends if they don't want to be! And so God must always leave
it possible for people to say No.

This is because he is a God of 'love'—the second word. Love doesn't kidnap people. Love respects freedom of choice. If God insisted that everyone should end up in heaven, irrespective of how we felt about it, that wouldn't be love. And also—love demands justice. It wouldn't be loving for God to make certain rules for the running of the universe—and then play fast and loose with them. If God has said, 'The soul that sins will die', he has to keep to his own decisions, however little he wants to. If he changed his mind every five minutes, and kept making exceptions, we wouldn't know where we stood. A universe run by an inconsistent, changeful God would be a terrifying place to live.

You see what we're saying? If God really is a God of love, it must always be possible for people to opt out of his plans and choose to go the wrong way. And if they do, God's love means that he can't just change the rules and let them off! They have to be freely able to choose to ignore God—and take the consequences.

What are the consequences? This is where we come to the word 'hell'. Most people associate hell with fire, sulphur, flames and burning. Why is this?

Well, it's because the word used for 'hell' in the New Testament—'Gehenna'—was the name of an actual place: the Valley of Hinnom, outside Jerusalem. Gehenna was the Jerusalem City Rubbish Dump. It was the place where you put objects which were of no further use to you—objects which had outlived any possibility of having a worthwhile function. And because Israel is a hot country, it wasn't a good idea to leave rubbish lying around to grow mouldy in the sunshine. So there was an endless fire burning in Gehenna, day and night, so that rubbish would be dealt with as soon as it was thrown there.

This is the reality of the picture the Bible paints of 'hell'. Hell is the rubbish dump. It is the place where God has to put people who have written themselves obstinately out of his plans for the universe—people about whom God has to say sadly, 'You have chosen to be of no further use to the future of creation. I have to respect your choice and put you away from my presence, where you have decided to go.' More than this we aren't told, about what hell is like; all those mediaeval pictures are pure imagination.

C. S. Lewis pictured hell as a grey, boring town in which dreary people lived who had no purpose or point in their joyless existence. Maybe; I don't know. All I know is that anyone who goes there will have chosen to do so by deliberately rejecting God's offer of new life.

But does it need to be 'for ever'? Well, remember that we are talking about a sphere outside time—where our normal understanding of the passage of days and years doesn't apply. Hell is like being frozen in time, permanently set in one particular moment. It isn't God's plan for any of us. But it is something he will *permit*—if we are stupid and independent enough to insist on it. A God of real love could do nothing else.

Do you find this a convincing answer?
☐ YES   ☐ NO   ☐ POSSIBLY

If you have further objections to the Christian view of LIFE AND DEATH, read some other parts of this section
(pp. 115–141)

Alternatively you may be asking:

Why worry now? I can get it all straightened out before I die   (Turn to p. 183)
If God knew we would make a mess of this planet, it was irresponsible of him to create it, wasn't it?
                                              (Turn to p. 18)

How can God condemn those who have never heard the Christian message?

As we have said already (p. 106), more people have heard—and responded to—the Christian message this century than ever before. But there are parts of the world where it is still unknown. What will God do about the tribes of headhunters in the Borneo jungle? It isn't their fault that they know nothing of Jesus Christ. And what about somebody who lives all his life in an atheistic country like Albania used to be, where the government openly boasts that all religion has been abolished? If God was fair, wouldn't he give the Albanian as many chances to decide about Jesus Christ as the Westerner who is brought up in Sunday school, exposed to RE lessons in school, and has a choice of twenty or so local churches to attend as an adult?

How can God send people to hell just because nobody ever told them?

Well, first, the Bible doesn't say that God does that. It insists that God is a totally fair and impartial judge, who does not play favourites—'There is no favouritism with God' is a statement that occurs no fewer than six times in the New Testament. However God judges (and we're not told many of the details), we can be sure he'll get the verdict right.

Second, God does not want anyone to be condemned. 'He is patient with you,' explains Peter, 'not wanting anyone to perish, but everyone to come to repentance.' In other words, if there is even the faintest chance of allowing someone to enter heaven, God will take it. The last thing he wants to do is to exclude anyone.

Third, just because people haven't heard the full story about Jesus Christ, it doesn't mean they have no awareness of God at all. When God put one man in Albania and another in Guildford, it was no mistake, according to the Bible: 'He determined the times set for them and the exact places where they should live. God did this so that men would seek him and perhaps reach out for him and find him, though he is not far from each one of us.' There are plenty of indications in the experience that every human has, that God exists and needs to be reckoned with.

What sort of indications? Well, there are two features which seem to be common to human beings in just about every civilization in the world's history. First, we all have an inbuilt sense of the supernatural, and even of a divine power—an awareness that there is someone who is bigger than we are (if you doubt this, look at p. 103). Second, we all have a conscience. We all believe that some things are right and other things are wrong.

And it is in the light of these two things that human beings will be judged, if they have not heard the Christian message. 'For,' says the Apostle Paul, 'since the creation of the world God's invisible qualities—his eternal power and divine nature —have been clearly seen, being understood from what has been made, so that men are without excuse.' Hearing about God's requirements helps to make it all much clearer—but just hearing isn't enough. 'For it is not those who hear the law who are righteous in God's sight, but it is those who obey the law who will be declared righteous.'

So—how will God judge those who haven't heard? Fairly and justly, without any penalties attached for ignorance. But maybe that's not the question you ought to be worrying about. For many of us, a much more important question is this one: How will God judge me if I *have* heard and still refuse to do anything about it?

Do you find this a convincing answer?
☐ YES   ☐ NO   ☐ POSSIBLY

If you have further objections to the Christian view of LIFE AND DEATH, read some other parts of this section
(pp. 115–141)

Alternatively you may be asking:

If God is so good, where did evil come from in the first place? (Turn to p. 147)
Aren't other sacred books just as valuable and true as the Bible? (Turn to p. 57)

Now that we can create life artificially, we have no need of God

Human engineering, genetic manipulation, test-tube babies, experiments on embryos—science has taken an amazing leap forward in our lifetime. Ideas that used to exist only in the wilder reaches of science fiction (cloning? genetic selection?) are now being seriously discussed as possibilities for the very near future.

We've never been able to create human life before. Our grandfathers thought only God could do that. Well—now that we can, do we need God any more? Aren't scientists 'playing God' quite successfully?

I think there are three reasons why God hasn't been superseded—and never will be. Here they are.

First, *we need God because 'creation' and 'procreation' are two different things*. Professor Donald Mackay has argued that what we human beings do is 'procreate'—we produce new human beings, whether through sexual reproduction or artificially in a test-tube. But we don't 'create'. We aren't responsible ultimately for holding the whole framework of being and existence in place. God does that.

When you watch a film on television, the actors in the film may seem to be totally responsible for their own actions, and (if it's a reasonably good film) everything they do will have a full, satisfying explanation in terms of the plot and their own motives. But at the same time someone right outside is 'holding them in being'—you! Because you have the power to switch them off by pressing a button!

In the same way, we can develop and manipulate all sorts of physical processes within this world system—and in fact the Bible tells us that God has commanded us to! But the whole show still depends on his creative control. 'Undertaken in the proper spirit,' observes Professor Mackay, 'human engineering is not playing God at all, but serving God: playing the man if you like; but not playing God.'[5]

Second, we need God because *every person is an individual*, with a significance and freedom given by God. Just because we can 'create life', it doesn't mean the people we produce are just puppets we can play about with. Every human being is unique, however he was brought to birth in the first place. Even if we could 'clone' people—that is, produce a new human being who was a perfect physical and mental copy of somebody who already existed—the 'clone' wouldn't be an identical dummy version of the original person. Because what makes a person or individual is the unique pattern of experiences and relationships which make up his life, and that can't be reproduced. The simple fact of biological likeness doesn't mean a loss of uniqueness or dignity. Every human being still stands apart from every other, and will only find the true satisfaction of his or her individual nature in a personal relationship with God, which fits the various parts of his life together and makes them make sense.

Third, we need God because science is a human business. It's wrong to think of science as an abstract, clinical affair conducted with total objectivity. Science is done by human beings, and so it involves human choices, value judgements, sometimes temptations. The results of science can be used for good or evil—to heal sick children or blow up cities. The kind of research done has to be chosen by people, and they may make the wrong choices—from reasons of pride, or stupidity, or greed, or inhumanity.

And our record so far shows that human beings are not very good at applying morality to science. Despite our stupendous discoveries, we are still selfish, greedy, conceited people. And the more we can do, through science and technology, the more damage we can cause! Man's biggest problem is himself. And on his own, he shows no signs of being able to solve that problem. He needs someone to come in from the outside and sort out his evil nature.

'No need of God'? I'd argue the opposite. I'd say we need God more desperately now, than ever we did before.

Do you find this a convincing answer?
☐ YES   ☐ NO   ☐ POSSIBLY

If you have further objections to the Christian view of LIFE AND DEATH, read some other parts of this section
(pp. 115–141)

Alternatively you may be asking:

But surely we don't need God in order to live a good life? (Turn to p. 167)

If God is the Creator, why does he allow natural disasters like volcanoes and earthquakes?

(Turn to p. 145)

Eternal life would be boring

One of the most potent myths in world literature is the story of the Wandering Jew—the legendary character who has been travelling wearily around the world for the last two thousand years, tired and aged, but totally unable to die. Living forever, the legend reminds us, may not be such a wonderful thing after all. You might reach the point very quickly where death would seem a blessed release. Nothing would be worse than being incapable of death.

And so when Christians talk excitedly about 'eternal life', and promote it as one of the great benefits of following Jesus, many people are not so sure. Who wants to live forever anyway? Wouldn't eternal life quickly become boring?

It's noticeable that this attitude is more common amongst younger people. Incidentally, the further you are from death, the less valuable life may seem! When she was a teenage singing sensation back in the Sixties, Cilla Black announced to the press that she wanted to die before she reached the age of forty. Watching her today, one can see that she's somehow managed to forget that particular ambition!

However, the question is still a fair one. Is eternal life such a good thing after all?

The first thing to notice is that the Bible doesn't talk about 'eternal life' as something that will happen in the future, but as something which is happening to Christians *here and now*:

Whoever believes in the Son has eternal life, but whoever rejects the Son will not see life . . .

> We know that we have passed from death to life, because we love our brothers . . .[6]

'Eternal life', in other words, isn't just an unnatural extension of existence beyond the grave. It's a whole new quality of life ('the life of eternity' might be a better way of translating the phrase) which can begin in someone's experience here and now, the moment he becomes a Christian, and will carry him right through death and out the other side. The emphasis isn't on the duration of it, but the quality of it. 'Eternal life' is an extra dimension in human living, the dimension that makes our whole experience fit together and become endlessly satisfying. The fact that it goes on for ever is of secondary importance!

Indeed, the Bible seems to indicate that you'll go on beyond the grave whether you are a Christian or not! The only question is whether you spend 'forever' in the exciting creativity and fulfilment of 'eternal life', or whether you opt out of God's plans forever:

> Then he will say to those on his left, 'Depart from me, you who are cursed . . .' Then they will go away to eternal punishment . . .[7]

Don't assume that living forever will be like an endless rainy weekend in Grimsby. For one thing, we're talking about a sphere right outside time, where normal conceptions of the passage of days and years just don't apply. We all know that if it were possible for someone to travel in a spaceship faster than the speed of light, he'd return to earth at a very different age than if he had remained on the earth's surface. But he wouldn't have felt any difference in the speed at which time had passed. It would just be that he had been in a realm where time worked differently.

For another thing, 'eternal life' doesn't necessarily mean complete absence of change—no variety, no surprises, no discoveries, no achievements. God has made us in such a way that we need the stimulation of challenges and explorations to keep us interested in life. Human beings are made for adventure. And if eternity includes everything that's best and most fulfilling for human life, it will include those things too.

Finally, even in everyday life there are 'signals of transcendence'—things we do that don't make sense unless there is another, external, realm of existence, outside time itself. The famous sociologist Peter Berger has written a book about this, called *A Rumour of Angels*. He claims that these are 'crucial dimensions of human life', and that to ignore them means 'the triumph of triviality'. We need to believe in eternal life if basic human activities are to have any point and meaning.

'Eternal life' is not a boring idea. It's exciting, fulfilling and vital if human life is to make sense. And if the Bible is right, you can have it now.

Do you find this a convincing answer?
☐ YES   ☐ NO   ☐ POSSIBLY

If you have further objections to the Christian view of LIFE AND DEATH, read some other parts of this section
(pp. 115–141)

Alternatively you may be asking:

But doesn't it make your life tame and uninteresting to be a Christian?   (Turn to p. 171)
But can't I get it all sorted out some time before I die?
(Turn to p. 183)

People have died and returned to life, but have never seen a heaven or hell

One of the most talked-about books of 1975 was *Life After Life*. Written by a doctor, Raymond Moody, it told the story of how over one hundred patients had experienced 'clinical death' on the operating table and had then been revived. And it claimed that in the midst of their traumatic experiences they had been on a journey to the after-death world and glimpsed life beyond the grave.

Dr. Elisabeth Kubler-Ross, who produced some of the research Moody used, wrote in the foreword to his book, 'It is research . . . that will enlighten many and confirm what we have been taught for two thousand years—that there is life after death.' But if Moody is right, the life after death is very different from what the Bible teaches about it.

One woman reported, 'I had always heard that when you died, you see both heaven and hell, but I didn't see either one.' Another commented, 'The strange thing was that I had always been taught in my religious upbringing that the minute you died you would be right at these beautiful gates, pearly gates. But here I was hovering around my own physical body, and that was it! I was just baffled.'

To be fair, the Bible doesn't promise visions of hell and heaven to the newly dead; nor does it teach the popular idea about flitting off on a cloud to stand before St. Peter at the pearly gates. But it does matter that so few of Moody's subjects reported any sense of judgement, punishment or reward; even before the Final Judgement, the Bible claims that there is a great gulf fixed between those whom God accepts and those who have rejected him. Has Moody disproved the Bible?

The first thing to notice is that there is no objective *evidence* that what these people have experienced is real. It has all happened in their heads. Thus although the experience may have been incredibly vivid and real to them, we can't prove that it was any more than a strange delusion which people encounter in that most distressing physical state. Obviously the descriptions have some imaginative content, anyway, since people from different religions have slightly different experiences to relate, coloured by what their upbringing conditioned them to expect. A Christian may meet Jesus in the next world; for a Hindu it's more likely to be Krishna; and so on.

Second, there may be good grounds for distrusting at least some of the evidence presented. The cases which Moody recounts were not his own patients. He gained a great deal from the work of Kubler-Ross, and she is a firm believer in life after death with some very odd ways of expressing her commitment. At one stage she was under investigation by the State of California for running a ranch at Escondido as a 'psychic brothel'; and she has written openly about how some of her information about the next world has come, not from scientific research, but from spirit communicators who materialized before her. When someone has such an obvious axe to grind, we'd be well advised to read her statements carefully.

Third, there can be perfectly reasonable alternative explanations for what happens in *Life After Life* experiences. Scientist Carl Sagan points out that the experience includes some features—for example being squeezed through a a long tunnel, and emerging into blazing light—which have already happened to us at one moment in our lives: the moment of birth. Is it possible that at our moment of greatest physical trauma, our mind flashes back suddenly to our previous most traumatic moment—when we emerged into the world for the first time? Except that now the memory has become jumbled with all sorts of theological ideas and hopes and fears about the next world, which our brain combines into an experience of life beyond the grave?

It's at least possible. And it is hard to see how Moody and his sympathisers could ever prove their case. The only way would be for someone who had really died, for an extended period, to return and give information to the rest of us. And the Bible claims that this is exactly what Jesus Christ did. We know he died, as a matter of historical fact, and the objective evidence for his resurrection (see p. 33) is far superior to anything Moody's book produces. So why should his ideas on the subject be less trustworthy than those of *Life After Life*?

Do you find this a convincing answer?
☐ YES   ☐ NO   ☐ POSSIBLY

If you have further objections to the Christian view of LIFE AND DEATH, read some other parts of this section
(pp. 115–141)

? *Alternatively you may be asking:*

Isn't Christianity just pie in the sky when you die?
(Turn to p. 149)
How could I be sure it was all true? (Turn to p. 180)

Human beings cannot be special because there must be millions of races like ourselves in our galaxy

We are very small. The universe is very big. We now know that we are living on just one planet of several which are whirling around the sun. And our solar system is just a tiny speck in a breathtakingly huge spiral, called a galaxy, which measures 100,000 light years from side to side.

These facts are humbling enough! But our galaxy is itself just a pinprick in the immensity of the universe, which contains innumerable galaxies no less important than ours. The furthest of them which we know about, called 3C–295, is all of 5,000 million light years away.

No wonder that many people conclude, 'With all those heavenly bodies circling around its's impossible that we are the only race in the universe. Other planets must be inhabited, too. And then where would that leave the Bible?'

Well, it's worth pointing out that the Bible never claims that we're on our own in space. It's certainly possible that other races exist, although there would be some interesting theological questions to work out in deciding how they fitted in to the scheme of things. But God could love and care for them just as genuinely as he loves and cares for us, without that fact making us any less 'special'.

When my second daughter was born, I grew to love her very much. But it didn't alter in any way the love, care and concern I felt for the daughter I already had! And when number 3 turned up—I was able to love her too, without loving the others any less.

Of course I had to give the other two less attention than

before, because I'm only a finite human being and I can't listen to three girls talking at once! But if I were infinite and could give three people my full attention simultaneously, then the older two wouldn't have suffered in that regard either.

Now God is infinite. One of the basic Christian beliefs about him is that he is capable of hearing the prayers, and answering the problems, of millions of different Christians all over the world, simultaneously. (If you think about it, it can't be too much of a problem to someone who is outside time anyway.) So he would be perfectly capable of caring for the details of the lives of different races on different planets in just the same way. But do these other races really exist?

Personally, I have to admit, I'm dubious. Wild claims have been confidently made in the past. It's not a hundred years since famous American astronomer Percival Lowell was asserting, 'Mars is inhabited by beings of some kind or other; this is as certain as it is uncertain what those beings may be.' But now we know that no life-forms like our own could exist on Mars, or indeed elsewhere in the solar system. The remainder of our system is a cold, lonely place. Is the rest of space like that?

We have had telescopes trained on the skies since 1948, listening for any hint of a coherent radio message from anywhere else. And we have heard nothing. Now our civilization is incredibly noisy; our television and radio transmissions can be detected light years away across space. If there were another civilization like ours anywhere within reach, it is incredible that we should have heard nothing from them.

The trouble is, we just can't assess what the chances are of a civilization coming into existence. We have only one case to judge from—ourselves! And this is the flaw in the famous Green Bank Formula, which is supposed to calculate that there must statistically be *millions* of races like ourselves. It depends for its validity on one vital factor, L—defined as the time-span within which a civilization will be able to communicate with other civilizations on other planets. Well, we've been able to do this for only a few years now; and we show no signs of coming to an end just yet (nuclear warfare permitting); so there's no basis for a calculation, and any estimate has got to be complete guesswork.

So there may be space beings or there may not. Either way, it doesn't affect the position of human beings before God: they are special, because they were created in God's image; special, because Jesus Christ gave his life for them; special because the chance of forgiveness and contact with the Creator is on offer to them right now.

Do you find this a convincing answer?
☐ YES   ☐ NO   ☐ POSSIBLY

If you have further objections to the Christian view of LIFE AND DEATH, read some other parts of this section (pp. 115–141). If you have read this whole section, go back to the START HERE page (p. 1) and choose another direction.

Alternatively you might be asking:

Is it really possible to see meaningful patterns in human history?   (Turn to p. 160)
Doesn't our scientific understanding of the universe's origins cast doubt on the idea of God?

(Turn to p. 7)

---

1. Quoted in Paul Davies, *God and the New Physics* (Harmondsworth, 1984), 84.
2. See Davies, *op. cit.*, 86.
3. See David Winter, *Hereafter* (London, 1972), 41–2.
4. Biblical quotations in this subsection are from 2 Peter 3:9; Acts 17:26–7; Romans 1:20; Romans 2:13.
5. D. M. Mackay, *Human Science and Human Dignity* (London, 1979), 59.
6. John 3:36; 1 John 3:14.
7. Matthew 25:41–6.

QUESTIONS ABOUT WORLD PROBLEMS AND TRAGEDIES

You have said that you agree with the statement

Christianity doesn't seem to me to make sense of the way the world is

This could be your opinion for several reasons. Here are some of the most common reasons people come up with. Tick whichever one(s) may apply to you.

☐ If God was really there he'd stop people
fighting   (p. 143)
☐ Why does God allow natural disasters like
earthquakes and volcanoes?   (p. 145)
☐ If the world was created by a good God, where
did evil come from?   (p. 147)
☐ Christianity is just pie in the sky when you
die   (p. 149)
☐ Why does God allow faithful believers to
suffer?   (p. 151)
☐ Why hasn't Christianity brought peace to the
world?   (p. 153)
☐ It's arrogant to believe human life matters in a
meaningless universe   (p. 155)
☐ Religion is just a distraction when there are
bigger problems to solve   (p. 157)
☐ It is impossible to see any patterns in history (p. 160)
☐ Answered prayer is just a delusion   (p. 162)

Now turn to the page(s) in this Section on which the answer is given to the statements you have ticked.

◀ Read them, and decide what you think of the answers
supplied. Then you can go back to the START HERE page
at the beginning of the book, and choose another direction.

▶ Or if you feel you've surveyed the evidence sufficiently already, turn straight to Section 9 (YOURSELF)—on p. 187—and follow the instructions there in order to check out your own position.

If God was really there he'd stop people fighting

The human record for violence certainly doesn't make a pretty story. Fifteen years of peace in the last two thousand. Twenty major wars since World War Two came to an end. Over 49.5 million people currently engaged in military activities around the world . . .

If there really is a God who wants peace and unity, why doesn't he do something? Why has he allowed the fighting to continue without taking some direct action?

To answer this question, we need to remember what sort of a world it is that God has actually created. He has created us as people—responsible individuals with the ability to make choices for ourselves. He could have made us plastic dolls or robots, and simply programmed us to do exactly as he said all the time, but he didn't. He entrusted us with a tremendous, awesomely valuable gift—freedom to choose.

(If he hadn't done this, incidentally, he wouldn't have been able to have a personal relationship with us; and this is what he wanted. It's like my relationship with my wife; she could have married someone else, and I could have chosen not to ask her to marry me, but we both chose each other, and that's what gives our marriage its magic. It wouldn't be quite the same if I had married a computerized robot, somehow. And in the same way God wanted us to be free to choose to have a relationship with him which would satisfy and complete our existence.)

The trouble is, as all these wars demonstrate, human beings keep making the wrong choice. We have turned our backs on God and tried instead to run this planet on our own. The result, inevitably, has been confusion, pain and heartbreak.

So what could God do to stop the wars?

I suppose there are four ways in which he could intervene. First, he could wipe us all out and start again. But he loves us too much to consider that possibility. As long as there's a chance of doing something with us, he won't wipe us out.

Second, he could simply re-programme our brains at a stroke; he could perform an instant lobotomy which would remove our aggressive instincts and make us automatically choose peace for the rest of our much-diminished lives. But this would mean taking away the precious gift of freedom he has given us. Instant lobotomies would produce a very neat, orderly, tidy planet. But also a very boring one. All individuality, all creativity, all sparkle would be gone from the race of obedient puppets once known as humankind.

Well, suppose he were simply to punish warfare as soon as it happened? So that everybody picking up a gun in anger was immediately zapped by a thunderbolt. Every general climbing into a jeep was instantly turned to a pillar of salt. Every tank in the world burst into flames as soon as someone tried to operate its guns . . .

People would get the message, very quickly, sure enough, and then there wouldn't be wars any more. But again God would have infringed our freedom. We might be peaceful now, because we'd be scared of the consequences of fighting; but our peacefulness wouldn't come from any internal motivation—it would be produced by pure fright. And if God wants us to be responsible moral beings, we need to be able to choose what's right for its own sake, not just because we're terrified of disobedience.

There is one other thing God could try. He could find a way for human beings to have their lives *voluntarily* transformed. A way for them to hand their whole being back to him, so that his Spirit could come and live inside them (yet without infringing their freedom to make their own decisions). A way in which he could work with them to produce the sort of character they should have had anyway, if they hadn't turned their backs on him and gone off in their own selfish direction. A way, in short, of changing human beings, one by one, from the inside out. And that—says the Bible—is exactly what he did.

⚖️ *Do you find this a convincing answer?*
☐ YES ☐ NO ☐ POSSIBLY

❗ *If you have further objections based on WORLD PROB-LEMS AND TRAGEDIES read some other parts of this section* (pp. 142–165)

❓ *Alternatively you might be asking:*

Why has Christianity started so many wars?
(Turn to p. 81)
Isn't the God of the Bible a bloodthirsty tyrant anyway?
(Turn to p. 12)

Why does God allow natural disasters like earthquakes and volcanoes?

A few years ago, several hundred people were attending a church in Italy. Praying to God. And what happened? God allowed an earthquake to erupt and destroy the very church in which they were singing his praises. Hundreds of people died. What sort of way is that for God to behave?

Many of the world's problems are caused by human wrongdoing; and God can't really be blamed for that. (Except, of course, that he created us to begin with—and we say more about that on p. 147). But many of our problems are not our own fault. Volcanoes, earthquakes, tidal waves, hurricanes, typhoons—why should God allow his world to be devastated by things like these? Does he enjoy watching human beings suffer? Or is he somehow powerless to stop it all happening?

The Bible traces natural disasters back to the Fall, the time when human beings first rebelled against God and disobeyed his instructions. As a result of the human attempt to hijack the planet, nothing has worked quite right since. In the Book of

Genesis, God warns Adam that now he has sinned life will not be so easy—the ground has been cursed, it will take 'painful toil' to make plants grow as they should, weeds will proliferate, men and animals will war on one another, women will suffer painful childbirth and sexual conflict will disfigure marriages. In other words, human rebellion has had its impact on every dimension of life on earth. It's as if the whole mainspring of creation has been broken, and although nature is still working, it is not working properly.

The Apostle Paul says that all of creation is 'groaning as in the pains of childbirth',[1] because things are not as they should be. Once I was driving along the road when all of a sudden my car started making an extremely strange noise. I stopped immediately and called for help. The patrolman who came told me that there was something seriously wrong with my car—that was why it was 'groaning as in the pains of childbirth'! And he advised me that I must not try to drive it an inch further. 'Every yard you go,' he said, 'you're hurting it a little bit more.'

Now my car still worked—after a fashion! I could have got it moving again, even though it would have been a noisy process! But I didn't dare, because I knew that even as it worked it would be damaging itself. And that's a little bit like the picture the Bible paints of this earth. It still works—but not properly. Volcanoes, earthquakes and the like were no part of God's original blueprint. They are just another demonstration that human sin has spoilt everything.

Can I prove it was human sin which produced natural disasters? No, of course not. But it is at least as good a theory as any other. When you are confronted with a world like ours—in which there are good bits (joy, creativity, satisfaction) and bad (frustrations, pain, disappointments, natural disasters)—you can come to any of three conclusions about it. You can conclude that the whole mess is just a complete accident; but as pp. 7–8 shows, that doesn't seem a very likely story. You can conclude that the world was actually created by an evil sadistic God, who likes viewing suffering; but you'd have even more problems explaining the existence of beauty and joy in a world built by a sadist, than you would explaining the existence of pain in a good God's world. Or, third, you can conclude that the world was indeed produced by a good God, but that it has been reduced to a mess by creatures to whom he gave some freedom. And that, it seems to me, covers more of the facts than either of the first two options.

Do you find this a convincing answer?
□ YES   □ NO   □ POSSIBLY

If you have further objections based on WORLD PROBLEMS AND TRAGEDIES read some other parts of this section *(pp. 142–165)*

Alternatively you might be asking:

If God made everything, who made God?
(Turn to p. 6)
Now that we can create life artificially, do we still need the idea of God? (Turn to p. 131)

If the world was created by a good God, where did evil come from?

All religions have to find some answer to the question of where evil came from. Some get round it by dualism, that is, by the idea that there are two creative forces, one good and the other evil, and they are engaged in a shoot-out for ultimate domination of the universe. So the good God is not responsible for evil; his opposite number created it . . .

It's an interesting theory. But it is one which Christianity cannot accept. Because Christians have always insisted that God created everything. He alone was there in the beginning. Nobody else lent a hand.

So does that mean God created evil?

St. Augustine tried to answer this question many centuries ago. And he pointed out that it's a mistake to think of evil as a 'thing'—like coal or wood or boiled rice. Evil is actually just an absence of something, a lack of what ought to exist. So it wasn't actually created as such. It was just there as the opposite of good.

As soon as you define what one thing is, you automatically create its opposite—out of what your definition excludes. The Welsh never thought of themselves as a nation, I'm told, until the English banded themselves together against the tribes who lived in Wales. Those who were excluded from the definition 'English' had to find a name for themselves . . . so they became 'Welsh'! The English never intended to create a rival nation who would beat them at rugby and inflict Welsh male voice choirs on the world. But by defining themselves, they created their opposite!

Do you see what we're saying? As soon as God defined what was good and acceptable to him, he left open the possibility of evil. Because as we've seen (p. 143) he created human beings with freedom to choose, and that meant giving them genuine alternatives to choose between. If human beings had been able to choose only what God wanted, that wouldn't have been freedom. (It would have been a bit like Henry T. Ford's famous line, 'You can have a car in any colour you like, as long as it's black!') So God did not create evil; but he created beings who had the potential to do evil.

The rest, as they say, is history.

Do you find this a convincing answer?
☐ YES   ☐ NO   ☐ POSSIBLY

If you have further objections based on WORLD PROB-LEMS AND TRAGEDIES read some other parts of this section   *(pp. 142–165)*

Alternatively you might be asking:

If God knew we would make a mess of this planet, was it irresponsible of him to create it?   (Turn to p. 18)
If God is a God of love, how does hell fit in?
(Turn to p. 127)

Christianity is just pie in the sky when you die

This famous phrase comes from a satirical song written by Joe Hill, the American social rights activist of the early twentieth century. Hill and his friends were fighting to free the working man from the exploitation of giant industrial combines. They were cynical about the empty promises of the preachers who tried to keep the workers happy with thoughts of heaven, but refused to help them practically:

You will eat, by and by,
In that glorious land above the sky,
Work and pray, live on hay,
You'll get pie in the sky when you die.

It may have been a fair criticism of the complacent religion they met in the factories and railroad camps of their period. But is it a just judgement of Christianity itself? Is the Christian faith no more than vague promises of 'pie in the sky'?

It's certainly true that the idea of heaven is an important one in Christianity. The early Christians looked forward to it with eager anticipation. It controlled their thoughts and their ambitions; they saw themselves in a new way because of it. 'Our Citizenship is in heaven,' wrote the Apostle Paul. 'And we eagerly await a Saviour from there, the Lord Jesus Christ, who, by the power that enables him to bring everything under his control, will transform our lowly bodies so that they will be like his glorious body.' Heaven seemed very close.

But that didn't mean that the Christians weren't interested in this present world. They did not allow themselves to become so fascinated with the next world that they shut themselves off from society in an artificial community. Christians were well known for their uncompromising social involvement (which we have written about on p. 72). They weren't other-worldly freaks, but on the contrary more truly and triumphantly alive than anyone else in the world. And this is what real Christianity will always be like: something which thrusts people forth into serving the world, and gives them new resources for coping with it.

What's more, although the Christians looked forward to a

glorious future, they insisted that their enjoyment of God's Kingdom had already started. It wasn't a case of 'Well, we must put up with trials and tribulations here, and somehow just keep on believing, because some day we'll have the last laugh'; it was a case of having there and then the first taste of what would eventually be something much bigger and much more satisfying. As we will see (p. 135) the Bible doesn't talk about 'eternal life' as a remote future possibility—but as something which can start right now and which produces an instant foretaste of heaven.

Some people simply assume that Christians see this world only as an ante-room for the next, a 'vale of soul-making' with no other function than to prepare us for heaven. But the Bible is enthusiastic about this world. It insists that 'everything God created is good, and nothing is to be rejected if it is received with thanksgiving'. Our purpose in being here is not to despise and deny ourselves the good things of life, but to enjoy the riches of creation as God intended we should. So it's not a waste of time for Christians to be involved in the arts, or in scientific research. Christians can legitimately enter parliament or run trades unions. Because their faith isn't 'pie in the sky when you die'. It's the only thing in the world which both enables and strengthens people to live in the here and now; and also leads them on to a future which will be far more glorious than anything they have dreamt of yet.

Do you find this a convincing answer?
☐ YES   ☐ NO   ☐ POSSIBLY

If you have further objections based on WORLD PROB-LEMS AND TRAGEDIES read some other parts of this section   *(pp. 142–165)*

Alternatively you might be asking:

But don't we come back for life after life?
                                              (Turn to p. 124)
Isn't the church just a money-spinning racket?
                                              (Turn to p. 71)

Why does God allow faithful believers to suffer?

Christians have never been promised an easy time. Right from the start of the Christian church—just a few years after Jesus had warned, 'All men will hate you because of me'—believers were being burned, flung to the lions, tortured and executed. Since those days, the list of Christians who have given their lives for their faith has lengthened with every century. Missionaries speared by cannibal tribesmen; Bible translators burned at the stake because of their desire to get God's Word to the people; doctors and pastors struck down by dreadful plagues because they refused to leave their post in times of epidemics. But why does God allow it? If these people are faithful followers of Jesus Christ, why doesn't he look after his own?

One answer is that God has made the universe to run by certain natural laws, and these laws operate in the same way for everyone. Jesus taught that God 'causes his sun to rise on the evil and the good, and sends rain on the righteous and the unrighteous'. If a Christian runs up against these natural laws in the wrong way, he is just as liable to be hurt as an unbeliever. For instance, a Christian who puts his finger into a live electricity socket cannot expect to be miraculously protected. A Christian who builds his house on the slopes of a volcano is taking as big a risk as any unbeliever.

If God changed the rules arbitrarily every time a Christian was liable to hurt himself, the universe would soon be in chaos. The whole system of science depends on order, design, repeatability. If rainclouds refused to release their load in case Christians got wet; if cars turned to jelly every time a Christian was involved in a road accident; if tornadoes suddenly changed their course to avoid Christians who were standing in the way—life would be impossible. The universe would be an unpredictable, capricious place, and nobody (apart from Christians!) would feel safe to go outside their doors. You'd never know what God might do next.

And thus, if you want to have a universe of regular natural law, you must expect it to be one where Christians will get hurt sometimes. In fact, Jesus never promised his followers free insurance, provided by management, against all the disasters of life. Quite the reverse; he warned quite realistically that following him meant a difficult time ahead. The way Jesus described the job prospects, nobody would have joined his movement simply for the fringe benefits!

In fact, Jesus knew that sometimes pain, stress and struggle are actually necessary experiences if life is to be all it should be. It is often in trying times that we learn the most important lessons, and get in touch with our feelings at the very deepest level. Looking back on my own life so far, I can think of a lot of fun times; they were enjoyable, of course, and I wouldn't have missed them for anything, but they didn't honestly benefit me much. The deepest and most precious experiences of my life are all associated with times of difficulty and pressure.

The Apostle Paul had a 'thorn in the flesh' (he doesn't state exactly what the problem was—it could have been anything at all) which he very much wanted God to take away from him. But God wouldn't. And in the end Paul came to see that God was allowing his suffering for a reason. He was teaching Paul invaluable lessons about God's faithfulness, and providing Paul with an understanding of God at such a deep level, that the Apostle wrote, 'Therefore I will boast all the more gladly about my weaknesses, so that Christ's power may rest on me. That is why, for Christ's sake, I delight in weaknesses, in insults, in hardships, in persecutions, in difficulties. For when I am weak, them I am strong.'[3]

Let's be honest. These are some reasons for the suffering which God allows even believers to go through; but they don't provide a complete explanation. There are still things we will never understand, events in which we will never see any meaning. But to a Christian who knows the daily reality of Jesus Christ by his side, the worst of inexplicable calamities can be bearable. God may not take Christians out of the disasters of life. But he takes them through them into a deeper and firmer confidence in himself; and at every step, every crossroads, he's there. All the time.

Do you find this a convincing answer?
☐ YES   ☐ NO   ☐ POSSIBLY

| ! | *If you have further objections based on WORLD PROBLEMS AND TRAGEDIES read some other parts of this section* (pp. 142–165) |

| ? | *Alternatively you might be asking:*

But can you really believe human beings are special to God, when there must be millions of races like ourselves in the universe? (Turn to p. 139)
Can Christians be sure they know God, or is it all wishful thinking? (Turn to p. 96) |

Why hasn't Christianity brought peace to the world?

'Glory to God in the highest,' sang the Christmas angels, 'and on earth peace to men'. Two thousand years later, the earthly side of this prediction hasn't yet come true. In fact, the coming of Christ has often been an excuse for wars instead. Christian versus infidel, Christian Brand X versus Christian Brand Y; why on earth hasn't Christianity brought peace to the world? Has it failed?

The first thing to notice is that Jesus never expected to bring peace to the world. 'Do not suppose that I have come to bring peace to the earth', he said. 'I did not come to bring peace, but a sword.'[4] He knew that his message would divide people who had formerly been the best of friends. Sons would fall out with fathers, daughters with mothers. 'A man's enemies will be the members of his own household.'

The second thing to notice is that, as we have seen (p. 143), God can't just step in and alter the processes of this world so that people won't fight any more. To do so would take away our freedom of choice. And so Christianity exists as God's answer to the problem of hatred and discord in the human heart; but God will not force anyone to accept it. If we choose to reject it, we can. And the result will be that strife will continue in the world.

The third thing to notice is that when someone becomes a Christian he receives God's Spirit, and that makes him place a new value on peace and peacemaking. I know a man who became a Christian in jail for wounding someone else almost fatally. His whole life to that point had been characterized by aggression and violence. Now, a gentler man-mountain you couldn't hope to meet. I know too a lad in Poland who fought policemen for the free trade union, Solidarity, during the riots of the early 1980s. His heart was full of hatred towards the men who were stifling his country. Now he's a Christian, he still wants free trade unions; he has kept all of his ideals intact; but the hatred has gone, and in its place there's a new unselfish caring spirit which just wasn't there before.

These internal character changes are the real achievements. Political negotiations can never bring about peace by themselves; all the strategic arms limitations talks will only lead to yet another set of strategic arms limitations talks. But when a man is rearranged in the very depths of his being, so that a new love and understanding starts to appear in everything he does—then something genuine has happened. 'God has poured out his love into our hearts,' says Paul, 'by the Holy Spirit, whom he has given us.'

And, finally, the Bible makes it clear that same day Jesus Christ will return in power to set all the wrongs of this earth right. Then, as never before, Christianity really will bring world peace. But until that happens, in the meantime, any individual who wants can take hold of God's offer of new life, and find the reality of the love of God for himself.

Do you find this a convincing answer?
☐ YES   ☐ NO   ☐ POSSIBLY

If you have further objections based on WORLD PROBLEMS AND TRAGEDIES read some other parts of this section (pp. 142–165)

? *Alternatively you might be asking:*

Isn't the church a device used by the rich to oppress the poor? (Turn to p. 69)
How do we know that Jesus wasn't just a lunatic?
(Turn to p. 42)

It's arrogant to believe human life matters in a meaningless universe

Correct. If the universe really is meaningless, human life is meaningless too. And it is therefore presumptuous to treat human life as if it's of any more value than the life of woodlice or caterpillars.

This, it seems to me, is the great problem for humanists and 'post-modernists'. They proclaim that there isn't any ultimate logic behind the universe, but they want us nevertheless to take human life very seriously indeed. They talk as if you can dismiss God and meaningfulness quite readily, and still leave human values unaffected. But is this right?

If the universe is meaningless, you can forget about love, for a start. Relationships between people have as little significance as the people themselves. For me to attach myself to another human being is really just weakness, because it opens up all sorts of possibilities of being hurt. No wonder that the songs of people who think this way focus so obsessively on broken, impermanent, fleeting relationships:

Travelling lady, stay a while
  Until the night is over.
I'm just a station on your way;
  I know I'm not your lover . . .[6]

Furthermore, you can forget about morality. There is no reason for saying that one action is more valuable that another one. You might just as reasonably help an old lady across the street—or blow her brains out with a revolver. Is this the message behind all the sudden violent images which keep cropping up in pop videos and trendy films by people like

Quentin Tarantino? That in our nightmare world anything goes, since morality has lost its value?

And as far as your own life is concerned, you can forget about any sense of purpose or achievement. Nothing you do will survive your lifetime. No action you take has any value. So whatever you do, you're going round in circles. Why bother passing exams, or working from nine to five? You might as well just amuse yourself and have a good time . . .

Those are a few of the implications of saying, 'We live in a meaningless universe.' And personally I'm not convinced that anybody can live with a philosophy of total meaninglessness. What people tend to do is to deny life is meaningful, and then smuggle in a belief in the meaning of certain bits of it ('. . . but I believe in love and honesty—they're really important . . .'). You have to find meaning somewhere; otherwise the only logical response is suicide. Aldous Huxley realized how unsatisfactory this smuggling process was:

> Meaning was reintroduced into the world, but only in patches. The universe as a whole still remained meaningless, but certain of its parts, such as the nation, the state, the class, the party, were endowed with significance and the highest value. The general acceptance of a doctrine that denies meaning and value to the world as a whole, while assigning them in a supreme degree to certain arbitrarily selected parts of the totality, can only have evil and disastrous results . . . [7]

Anyway, if you are going to say, 'Everything is meaningless', notice what happens. Your statement becomes meaningless too! So why should you believe it? And now we're going round in circles. Albert Camus realized this problem. 'I proclaim that I believe in nothing,' he reflected, 'and that everything is absurd, but I cannot doubt the validity of my own proclamation and I am compelled to believe, at least, in my own protest.'[8] Hardly a very logical or consistent position.

These are some of the difficulties of trying to make anything mean anything when you start from the position that the universe is meaningless. But why should you start from that position? In this book we've tried to show that there is plenty of evidence for design and planning in the way the universe is put together (p. 7). That Jesus Christ may well have been exactly who he claimed to be, and that if so life does have a meaning (pp. 23, 33, 35). That an experience of the reality of God needn't just be a psychological trick (p. 92) or wishful thinking (p. 96). And a few pages on, you will see that it isn't ridiculous to believe that there is a God in charge of history (p. 160) or that he answers prayers in a coherent, observable way (p. 162).

Often people say, 'Oh, I think the universe is meaningless', because that allows them to ignore the tricky questions that crop up when you have to take the existence of God into account. But this attitude flies in the face of the evidence. And believing in 'meaninglessness' leaves you with more questions than it answers!

Do you find this a convincing answer?
☐ YES ☐ NO ☐ POSSIBLY

! *If you have further objections based on WORLD PROBLEMS AND TRAGEDIES read some other parts of this section* (pp. 142–165)

? *Alternatively you might be asking:*

If God is really there, why doesn't he do miracles today? (Turn to p. 178)
The idea of evolution has made the idea of God impossible—hasn't it? (Turn to p. 9)

Religion is just a distraction when there are bigger problems to solve

It is said that while the invading Turkish army was battering at the gates of Constantinople, theologians inside the city were meeting for an urgent conference. And the subject they were so keenly discussing was: How many angels can stand on the head of a pin?

The story may or may not be true. But it demonstrates graphically the objection many people have to religion. It's an other-worldly distraction. It takes your attention away from the actual, immediate problems of your situation, and envelops you in a cosy never-never land where God's in his heaven and all's right with the world. What good does it do to pray in churches when millions of the starving are waiting to be fed? Why should theologians deliver learned papers to one another about the Christian concept of sacrificial love, when they could use the same amount of energy in actually showing love to needy people within society? Was Karl Marx right when he claimed that religion was something fed to the masses like a drug, to make them quietly accept injustice, and not try to claim their fundamental human rights? Is religion just a distraction from the problems we need to solve?

It would be interesting to discuss what the biggest problems of society actually are. But we have no space to do that here, so let's just assume we know already. How are we going to solve them? I'd say you need three things: a goal to aim for; standards to operate by; and the power to bring about your aims. And I would say you'll find it hard to achieve any of these things without religion.

First, you need *an overall goal to aim at*. What kind of society do you really want to produce? Your ideas will be coloured by your basic beliefs about the significance of human life, the importance of the individual, and the ways in which you think human beings ought to act towards one another. Now, as we've already seen (p. 155), it is hard to maintain a belief in the significance of human life if you've rejected religion and concluded that the world is basically meaningless. It was the idea that life is ultimately without value that led to the horrors of the Terror in France, the bloodbath of Cambodia, the Gulag Archipelago. Revolution led all three countries to lose their moorings in sanity, and drift into a nightmare of illogicality —because their goal wasn't securely based.

Also you need *standards to operate by*. How will you bring about your goal for society? Is lying all right? How about cheating, stealing, a little discreet murdering here and there—provided they bring about the result you want? We've already mentioned (p. 155) that people who turn their back on the possibility of a religious dimension have great difficulty in saying why human beings should act morally, or which moral code they ought to adopt. There are no absolute values on which to base morality. So it becomes acceptable to send six million Jews to their death, if it will bring about the triumph of the Third Reich; it is reasonable for murder squads to stalk the streets of Chile; it is just firm government to torture the enemies of the state in a grim building in Kampala. No religion—no reason for morality either.

Finally, and most crucially, you need *the power to bring about what you want to achieve*. There have been endless schemes for perfecting this planet, ending injustice and bringing about equality—and they have all (even the Marxist attempts) failed completely. The problem they all run up against is that human beings are imperfect. They are not always altruistic, not always selfless, not always noble and heroic. Inside every one of us is the principle which the Bible calls 'sin', the hidden bias in human nature which pulls us off course again and again, and ensures that we can never live up to the standards we know we ought to embrace.

The only way in which you will change the world is to change people first. To bring about an inner transformation that turns their selfishness into idealism, their greed into a readiness to share. And here most religions can't help you much. But there is one, as we've seen already (p.103), which claims to turn people into 'new creations' who are 'born again' with 'a pure heart and a good conscience and a sincere faith'. These people have been prominent for two thousand years in all the reforming, caring movements of the world (see p. 71). They alone have what society needs.

We can solve our problems without Christianity? It's just a distraction from reality? Certainly not. Christianity is the only way to the reality society needs to find.

🜲 *Do you find this a convincing answer?*
   ☐ YES   ☐ NO   ☐ POSSIBLY

❗ *If you have further objections based on WORLD PROB-LEMS AND TRAGEDIES read some other parts of this section*   *(pp. 142–165)*

? *Alternatively you might be asking:*

Surely we don't need God in order to live a good life?
(Turn to p. 167)
Aren't people too sophisticated nowadays to be religious?   (Turn to p. 101)

It is impossible to see any patterns in history

History, said H. A. L. Fisher, is just 'one damn fact after another'. More elegantly, he wrote, 'Men wiser and more learned that I have discerned in history a plot, a rhythm, a predetermined pattern. These harmonies are concealed from me. I can see only one emergency following upon another as wave follows upon wave.'[9]

Is that all history is—a meaningless jumble of events? Or is it possible, as the Bible claims, that God is at work in history, and his hand can be seen guiding some of the things that happen?

It is important to notice what the Bible does not claim. First, it does not claim that God's actions in history will be dramatic interventions that suddenly suspend the laws of nature and make things happen in a way which would never have naturally occurred. God doesn't work against natural processes, in spite of them but through them. So when the Bible says 'God hardened Pharaoh's heart', it doesn't mean that the King of Egypt suddenly and inexplicably became stubborn and unreasonable when least expected to. In fact, it was psychologically quite probable that he would become difficult to deal with, and all that the Bible is saying is that God worked through these natural processes of feeling and reacting to bring about the conclusion God intended.

Then again, the Bible does not claim that all God's actions in history will be easy to spot. There may be things which stick out as clear examples of his grace or his judgement—as far as a believer can see; but there will be other times when the whole process is shrouded in mystery. The prophets of Israel were often not at all sure why God was doing the things he was doing. (Look at Habakkuk, for example, who wrestles with the problem of why God seems to be acting in the opposite way from what was needed at that time in history.) But they were convinced that, whether human beings could see it or not, God was at work in history, guiding the course of human events, sustaining, helping and judging.

Third, the Bible does not claim that every specific thing that happens has an immediate moral significance. In other words, God is not necessarily speaking to us through every trivial incident that takes place. Jesus made this point when he was told about a disaster which had happened to some men in the neighbourhood. He answered, 'Do you think they were more guilty than all the others living in Jerusalem? I tell you, no!'[10] Their deaths were not to be seen as punishment from God. The meaning of the event lay deeper than that.

So God's way of acting in history doesn't ride roughshod over normal probabilities or historical mechanisms. God's activity employs those natural processes to bring about his will. This means that you may be able to find convincing reasons for everything that occurred in one historical episode—psychologically, culturally, politically—and still not have exhausted the significance of it. For there is another dimension to be remembered as well, God's purposes in it.

Therefore the believer will see an extra level in history that the unbeliever won't. Dr. E. W. Ives, Senior Lecturer in History at Birmingham University, expresses it like this:

> Just as a divine plan in human events is not perceptible to historical enquiry, neither is the significance which the prophet sees in this event or that. The believer who asks the historian, 'Don't you think that God is judging . . .?' can only receive the answer 'Not from my point of view'. It is possible to analyze a picture in scientific terms—as paint; it is also possible to analyze the same picture in artistic terms—as a painting. According to tbe way we organize knowledge today, the two descriptions will be complementary but separate; each will be completely valid and each will be distinct from the other.[11]

Can you prove the extra dimension is there? No, of course you can't. But you can demonstrate that it isn't ridiculous to believe it's there!

⚖️ *Do you find this a convincing answer?*
   ☐ YES   ☐ NO   ☐ POSSIBLY

❗ *If you have further objections based on WORLD PROB-
   LEMS AND TRAGEDIES read some other parts of this
   section*   *(pp. 142–165)*

❓ *Alternatively you might be asking:*

   Haven't archaeological discoveries exploded many of
   the Bible's claims about history?   (Turn to p. 59)
   Are human beings really anything more than sophisticated machines?   (Turn to p. 116)

Answered prayer is just a delusion

Isn't it a bit like believing in fairy stories, to say that God
answers our prayers? Doesn't it turn him into a Fairy
Godmother, a heavenly Father Christmas dispensing goodies?

Christians have never thought so. Christians have always
claimed that God meets their needs and listens to their
requests.

The New Testament insists, 'Do not be anxious about
anything, but in everything, by prayer and petition, with
thanksgiving, present your requests to God.' If you find that
ridiculous, you probably have one of three different kinds of
objection to the whole idea.

Some people have *philosophical* objections to the idea of
answered prayer. They argue that if God exists he must be far
too immense to be bothered about providing good weather for
the Sunday school picnic. Associating God with our petty,

local worries and needs is reducing him to something trivial, parochial, almost cosy.

But surely this is to fall into the very modern trap of assuming that something big and important must be bureaucratic. It's certainly true that in the world of government and business, the more important an official is, the less time he will have for individual people and tiny concerns. But the very greatness of God is that while he's big enough to hold all the worlds together he's also concerned enough to listen to the smallest request from the least of his children. Jesus remarked that not even a sparrow dropped down and died without God's being aware of the fact.

So it isn't ridiculous to ask God to help Mrs. Jones not to suffer too much with her chilblains. If he had any less concern and knowledge about Mrs. Jones' situation than he has about the precise trajectory of the planet Jupiter, God would not be God.

Second, some people have *moral* objections. Why should God play favourites? Why should one specially blessed group of human beings have a hot line to heaven, enabling them to call on God for supernatural assistance when most of the human race has to get by on its own?

There are two answers to this. First, the Bible makes it clear that God's favour and ready ear are available to everyone who is willing to turn to him in faith. The very first passage quoted in the very first Christian sermon of all time says: 'Everyone who calls on the name of the Lord will be saved.'

Second, prayer is not just a divine shopping list in which we focus exclusively on our own needs and wants. Christians are told to pray for others—for friends and relatives, for Christians at work all over the world, for kings and governmental authorities. Any Christian whose prayers are all (or even mainly) about himself hasn't even started to discover what prayer is really about. Prayer can be a channel to bring God's help into other people's situations of need—not just our own.

Finally, some people have *practical* objections. 'It doesn't work.' Well, it's true that God doesn't say Yes every time. And it's good that he doesn't; if he had granted my requests at first time of asking, I'd have been married to the wrong girl, doing a totally unsuitable job, and living in the wrong part of the country! Looking back now at what I thought was right for myself, I can see that my original ideas would have been disastrous. I'm grateful to God for not giving me what I thought I wanted!

But in my experience God says Yes far too often for it to be simple coincidence. If you came down from bed one morning to find the freezer door standing open, you might just conclude it had been left open by chance, and shut it, thinking no more about it. But if you found the same thing happening every day for a week, you would find it hard to believe that it was 'just chance' any more! You might start to suspect that a junior member of your family was getting out of bed and helping himself regularly. In the same way, without becoming superstitious about it, I believe I have seen too many clear-cut examples of God intervening and answering my prayers to doubt him any longer. It does work. It is real.

Maybe if you're still uncertain there will be only one way for you to find out. Which will be: to enter on a relationship with God for yourself. And experience in your own life just how ready he is to answer your prayers.

Is there any good reason why you shouldn't?

Do you find this a convincing answer?
☐ YES   ☐ NO   ☐ POSSIBLY

If you have further objections based on WORLD PROBLEMS AND TRAGEDIES read some other parts of this section (pp. 142–165). If you have read this whole section, go back to the START HERE page (p. 1) and choose another direction.

Alternatively you might be asking:

But surely you can't accept literally what the Bible says, in this day and age?   (Turn to p. 61)
But would I be good enough for God to accept me?
                                                      (Turn to p. 185)

1. See Genesis 3:17–19 and Romans 8:19–22.
2. Matthew 10:22.
3. 2 Cor. 12:9–10.
4. Matthew 10:34.
5. Romans 5:5.
6. Leonard Cohen, 'Travelling Lady', copyright MAM Publishing Inc.
7. Aldous Huxley, *Ends and Means*, quoted by Colin Chapman, *Christianity on Trial* (Berkhamsted, 1974), 105.
8. Albert Camus, *The Rebel* (Harmondsworth, 1967), 16.
9. H. A. L. Fisher, preface to *History of Europe* (London, 1936).
10. Luke 13:2–3.
11. E. W. Ives, *God in History* (Tring, 1979), 72.

QUESTIONS ABOUT BEING A CHRISTIAN

You have said that you agree with the statement

Being a Christian doesn't seem like a possible life for me

This could be your opinion for several reasons. Here are some of the most common reasons people come up with. Tick whichever one(s) may apply to you.

☐ We don't need God in order to live a good life (p. 167)
☐ It's impossible to change yourself in order to
 please God (p. 169)
☐ Being a Christian makes your life tame and
 uninteresting (p. 171)
☐ Christians are obsessed with saving their own
 souls at the expense of the world (p. 173)
☐ Christian standards in sex and marriage are
 impossible for most people (p. 175)
☐ How come God doesn't do miracles today? (p. 178)
☐ How could I be sure it was all true? (p. 180)
☐ Christians all look alike—and I couldn't be like
 that (p. 182)
☐ I can get it all straightened out before I die (p. 183)
☐ I'm not good enough for God to accept me (p. 185)

Now turn to the page(s) in this Section on which the answer is given to the statements you have ticked.

◀ Read them, and decide what you think of the answers
 supplied. Then you can go back to the START HERE page
at the beginning of the book, and choose another direction.

Alternatively you might be asking:

But aren't some people naturally 'religious' and others not? (Turn to p. 99)
Can't I worship God without needing to belong to a church? (Turn to p. 75)

Being a Christian makes your life tame and uninteresting

Who wants to be a pale, spotty adult version of the Milky Bar Kid, interested only in building models of Westminster Abbey out of matchsticks, garbed dreadfully in clothes that a charity shop would have turned down back in the sixties, off to bed every night at nine-thirty with a cup of cocoa and a digestive biscuit? Not many of us, probably. Yet this is the idea of Christianity that many people carry round in their heads . . .

Where did they get it from? Well, let's admit quite openly that there are boring, tame people in the church. There are also exciting, lively people in the church. Neither side has a monopoly; Christianity is for everyone, not just one type of disposition. You can understand the appeal of Christianity to people who want to find safety, peace and security; no wonder tame people join. Mind you, God has a way of stretching them and changing them when he gets hold of them—putting them through alarming adventures, giving them more confidence in themselves and others, helping them to blossom as personalities. God loves dull people, but he doesn't want them to stay that way.

We have to make another admission. There are even people who were once quite lively but have become tame and uninteresting by becoming Christians. This should not happen. But it does, sometimes; because they become so absorbed in their new life that they drop all the previous activities which made up their life, see less of their friends, spend their days in a monochrome world of prayer meetings and hymn singing sessions. God does not intend us to become spiritual freaks,

and such people are just temporarily unbalanced. They tend to
adjust again after a while; but meanwhile, unfortunately,
others may have got the message, 'So that's what Christianity
does to you. No thanks!'

If you really think that 'being a Christian makes your life
tame and uninteresting' I think that maybe one of four things
is true of you. First, maybe you have yet to meet any
interesting Christians! If I could introduce you to Brian
Greenaway—who used to be President of a chapter of Hell's
Angels—or Jim Wallis—a social rights activist with a passion-
ate Christian commitment which has got him into trouble with
the law more than once—you would be unlikely to find them
'tame'!

Second, maybe you don't know what Christians can do. Life
is not a narrow round of Bible conferences and choir practices!
Every year at the Greenbelt Festival (see pp. 88–89) I meet
scores of wide-eyed, shocked non-Christians who have
naively assumed that Christians are forbidden to get involved
with any activity not specifically mentioned by name in the
Book of Leviticus. And surrounded by the riot of colour,
exuberance and creativity that makes up a youthful Christian
festival, they have to rub their eyes in disbelief.

Third, maybe you are confusing pleasure with fun. It isn't
true that certain activities automatically lead to having fun—or
that you can't have fun without them. You can spend your
whole life in pursuit of pleasure without actually enjoying any
of it. Jesus Christ adds a new dimension to living which means
that every part of your life—not just the pleasure-seeking
bits—takes on a new, enhanced quality. So you don't need to
go out and get drunk, or chase women, or gorge yourself silly
while the rest of the world is starving. These things will
probably not be much fun anyway in the end; real contentment starts with Jesus.

Fourth, maybe the Christian life seems dull because you
don't yet understand what Christians enjoy. Nobody in his
senses wants to spend time in a prayer meeting—if all that
happens is that you shut your eyes meekly and sit on a bench
for half an hour. But if you are a real Christian, and prayer
means talking to God, and you know you may emerge from
the meeting having actively influenced situations thousands of
miles away around the world—or having met God in a new

way, so that you 're shaken rigid by the joy and holiness of his presence—suddenly it's not so boring!

Being a Christian makes your life tame and uninteresting? You have no right to make that charge until you've tried it out for yourself. But then you'll know better!

Do you find this a convincing answer?
☐ YES ☐ NO ☐ POSSIBLY

If you have further objections to the idea of BEING A CHRISTIAN, read some other parts of this section
(pp. 166–186)

Alternatively you might be asking:

Aren't most people too sophisticated nowadays to be religious? (Turn to p. 101)
Isn't it true that what the church does is boring and outdated? (Turn to p. 88)

Christians are obsessed with saving their own souls at the expense of the world

We live in a world that is desperately sick. There are so many problems to be solved, so many situations of need to be met, that quite literally every second counts. Even if we could solve the hunger problems of Africa by midnight tonight, that would be too late to prevent the deaths of thousands of children. Every minute the world spends another half million dollars on armaments. Every second counts.

And so people who realize the extent of our problems, and feel committed to be working for a solution, often get quite angry with Christians. These church people—they claim to be concerned, but why do they waste so much time? What's the point in praying, singing hymns and trying to convert the neighbours when there are more important things to do? Isn't it selfish to spend time worrying about whether you will get into heaven, when others have much more pressing problems you could be helping with?

We've already answered part of this question (p. 157). It isn't a case of 'either . . . or'. If the Bible is right in claiming that the fundamental problems of the world come from human rebellion against God, then the most important thing to do is to put people back into the right relationship with God once again. You can try to feed the hungry or stop the arms race, without dealing with human selfishness and hostility to God's plans, but you'd be treating the symptom and leaving the disease untouched. Like putting a sticking plaster on top of gangrene.

So helping people to discover a relationship with Jesus Christ is in fact one important way of making a full-frontal attack on the desperate sickness of this planet. But I'm not saying that we have only to preach the word, and lo, all our problems will vanish, just like that. Christians must get involved in practical action to alleviate distress and fight oppression too. The Christian message isn't complete unless the 'new life' it produces radically alters a person's involvement with his society.

Before his death in a road accident, David Bosch was a quiet middle-aged university professor in South Africa who had obstinately turned down the chance to move to safer, better-paid jobs in America during the *apartheid* years—because he felt God wanted him to stay in his own troubled country and work for justice there. He argued that Christians should not just sit back and wait for the end of the world, but 'prepare for the end by being involved in the here and now. The world may indeed be enemy-occupied territory but the enemy has no property rights in it. He is a thief and a liar. Our responsibility is to be good stewards of the King. We may not therefore be indifferent to the way the world is governed, nor to the injustices that appear to be endemic in it.'

If 'salvation' leads us to an obsessive, neurotic concern with ourselves, it isn't salvation. If it broadens our horizons and enlarges our sympathies for others, we have found the real thing.

The record of the church through the ages demonstrates this. Father Damien, Thomas Barnardo, George Muller, William Wilberforce, and so many thousands of other unsung heroes—people who discovered that belonging to Christ wasn't a safe retreat from the troubles of the world, but something which thrust them out into active sacrificial service for other human beings. That's real Christianity.

Do you find this a convincing answer?
☐ YES   ☐ NO   ☐ POSSIBLY

If you have further objections to the idea of BEING A CHRISTIAN, read some other parts of this section
(pp. 166–186)

Alternatively you might be asking:

If the world was created by a good God, where did evil come from anyway? (Turn to p. 147)
Hasn't Christianity been starting wars for centuries? (Turn to p. 81)

Christian standards in sex and marriage are impossible for most people today

This is a subject which requires a whole book to answer. (And there are some good ones; you could try Lewis Smedes, *Sex in the Real World* (Lion) or John White, *Eros Defiled* (IVP) if you want some more to think about) but we need to say a little about it here because this is such a major area of misunderstanding for so many people. Since the sexual revolution of the sixties, Christian ideas about sex and marriage have gained the reputation of being repressive, unrealistic, narrow-minded and joyless. Do they still make sense today?

People who say 'No' often feel, 'Christian standards are impossible for us because we are more liberated now.' But it's a question of what you mean by 'liberated'. Is there really more freedom in sex without commitment—no deposit, no return relationships, in which either partner can move off at a moment's notice? Hasn't the married partner more freedom: freedom from comparison with rivals for your lover's affections; freedom to grow old, secure in a love which will not end as soon as your charms fade; freedom to enjoy total intimacy with another person, without fear of an abrupt ending; freedom to be natural with the other sex, knowing that friendliness is much less likely to be misinterpreted as a chat-up? Freedom to say No to sex occasionally without feeling that you may lose the relationship unless you give in?

Shere Hite's *The Hite Report* found that women often felt better for holding back from sex for a while; to their surprise, they didn't really need it as much as they had assumed. Says Dr. Joyce Brothers:

> The pressure from the culture is strong not to be chaste. People simply feel about as satisfied after casual, perfunctory sex, as after a sneeze—a momentary release of tension, that's all. There is a great deal of evidence that when youngsters involve themselves too early in sex they never learn to fuse love and sex and it remains two separate things. One is physically ready to have sex much earlier than one is ready emotionally . . .[4]

Is 'liberation' really freedom—or just another way of tying yourself up in chains?

Sometimes, too, people think, 'The Bible was written centuries ago. We know more now.' About the physiology of sex, yes. About how to achieve the perfect orgasm, possibly. But about relationships? And the pain of guilt, betrayal, jealousy? We have just as much heartbreak and disillusion as ever there was. We can describe what goes on in sex, clinically, and illustrate it with colour photographs. Masters and Johnson, Kinsey and Comfort, have increased our awareness of what happens; but we're no better at making it work emotionally. Even a sex goddess like Marilyn Monroe once confessed to a sexual partner that she was never sure she was doing it properly . . .

This is where the Bible's incisive understanding of human nature, and its clear rules for faithfulness and dependability, can still form a solid foundation for sexual relationships in our century. And don't assume Bible writers knew nothing about sex, either. Many standard textbooks on venereal disease mention Moses as an unbelievably progressive Medical Officer of Health, in view of the rules he laid down for Israelite sexual practice. He seems to have been centuries ahead of his time. But then he claimed that God had told him what to do.

Finally, people sometimes object, 'But we are more under-standing now.' Since the Kinsey Report, we know that there are many more homosexuals than anyone had imagined; surely we should just live and let live. Since Victorian hypocrisy has disappeared, we know that people often do sleep around and have affairs; surely it's only human, and we shouldn't judge too harshly. But homosexual experience is only a pale caricature of what God intended sex to be, and Christians who have battled with homosexual impulses (and in some cases lost them completely) have found much more fulfilment in facing the challenge of Christian living than in going along with the unsatisfying half-world of the gay scene. And thanks to our 'understanding' attitude to irregular sexual liaisons, we have a sophisticated culture crippled by fear of AIDS and herpes; unable to hold its marriages together (on current figures, over one in three is ending in divorce); and obsessed by sex, but unable to find real contentment within it.

Christian standards are not impossible today. In fact, there's not much else around that works—is there?

Do you find this a convincing answer?
☐ YES ☐ NO ☐ POSSIBLY

If you have further objections to the idea of BEING A CHRISTIAN, read some other parts of this section
(pp. 166–186)

Alternatively you might be asking:

But aren't human beings just sophisticated machines
anyway?   (Turn to p. 116)
But hasn't Christianity always been male-dominated
and unfair to women?   (Turn to p. 85)

Why doesn't God do miracles today?

Wouldn't it be easy to believe, if you saw water turned into
wine? Or lame people healed in an instant? Or five loaves and
two fish feeding five thousand people?

Or would it?

The interesting thing about Jesus' miracles was that they led
some people to belief. And left some other people uncon-
vinced. In other words, if you were ready to believe, the
miracles formed an additional piece of evidence that helped
you reach the right conclusion. But if you were determined
already that Jesus had to be an impostor or a rogue, all the
miracles in the world wouldn't make any difference.

Miraculous events often don't convince people—because
they find it hard to trust the evidence of their own eyes. Often
they are reluctant to admit to themselves that anything has
really happened. We have been studying parapsychology for
over fifty years now as a university discipline, and despite
decades of tests costing millions of dollars people are still
arguing about whether extra-sensory perception exists or not!
That's how difficult it is for us to make up our minds about
phenomena which are bizarre and outside our normal
experience.

A few years ago, at Garabandal in Spain, a young girl
claimed to have had a vision of the Virgin Mary. Many people
believed her, and a new church has been built, thousands of
pilgrims visit the spot every year, and some tour companies
make their money exclusively by running trips to Garabandal.
Yet the young girl herself is now unsure whether or not she
genuinely did have a vision—or whether she dreamt it. The

experience was so unusual that, although at the time she was convinced, now she is much less sure. Miraculous events don't necessarily provide conclusive proof of anything.

And that, I think is one reason why there are fewer miracles today than happened in the time of Jesus. His miracles were a kind of megaphone drawing attention to the way God was at work, and to the claims of Jesus, demonstrating graphically his power and his concern for human misery. But they were not conclusive proof, automatically accepted by everybody. Jesus told a story about a man who died and found himself facing God's punishment. This man begged for someone to go to earth and supernaturally warn his brothers not to fall into the same fate. But the answer he received was terse and realistic: 'If they do not listen to Moses and the Prophets, they will not be convinced even if someone rises from the dead.'[5]

This is why it doesn't make sense to argue, 'If God wants me to believe in him, he'll have to work a miracle. I will believe in him only when he does something indisputable.' Because miracles aren't indisputable; and anyway what right have you got to hold God to ransom in this way?

Finally, don't assume that there are no miracles, and haven't been for two thousand years! People are still healed, suddenly and dramatically, today. Those who have had deep, dark oppressions and behaviour problems in their lives, caused by supernatural evil, are restored to health. Christian workers who are in desperate need of some piece of equipment, or a specific sum of money, still find God answering their prayers in unforeseeable and incredible ways. God is still very much in business.

And the greatest miracle of all happens when a human life is opened up to allow Jesus to take control. Thinking back over ex-drug abusers, murderers, thieves and desperate potential suicides I've known, who have come to know Jesus and have found a new dimension to life through him, the question starts to sound more and more silly. 'Why doesn't God do miracles today?' Whatever made you think he'd stopped?

Do you find this a convincing answer?
☐ YES   ☐ NO   ☐ POSSIBLY

| ! | *If you have further objections to the idea of BEING A CHRISTIAN, read some other parts of this section*
 (pp. 166–186) |

| ? | *Alternatively you might be asking:* |

But can you believe in the miracles of Jesus today?
(Turn to p. 29)
Does God really answer people's prayers, or is this just a delusion?   (Turn to p. 162)

How can I be sure it was all true?

For many people, this is the Number One problem. They can see that there is good evidence supporting Jesus' claims. They can understand why the Bible's ideas about human life make sense. They have noticed a change for the better in the lives of friends who have become Christians. But how can they be sure? Might it not all just be a plausible fantasy?

Two things are obvious. First, you need more than just a convincing argument. I have a friend who is a maths teacher, who has shown me three ways of proving by algebra that two equals one. Now we all know that this is rubbish, but nonetheless the calculation is extremely convincing. There's a tiny hidden error in it, but it's so plausible that you might never notice. Similarly, if I tried to make you sure of God's existence by giving you some abstract arguments, it wouldn't be enough. Your mind would never be quite at rest. You would spend the rest of your life looking for the flaw in the calculation.

But second, you need more than an experience or a feeling. Miracles and bizarre experiences don't prove anything (we have talked about this on p. 178). If God suddenly manifested before you on a flaming cloud, you might be impressed and overawed at the time. You might feel thoroughly convinced.

But half an hour later you might be asking yourself, 'Was it real? Did it happen? Was it a hallucination? Did I just go mad for five minutes?' You'd never be sure.

Or you might wake up in the morning with an odd, choking feeling in your heart that Jesus was God. You just know it's true. Would that be convincing enough? No, because feelings can be deceptive; Hitler 'just knew' six million Jews had to die; the Yorkshire Ripper 'just knew' he had to murder prostitutes. People like that may be totally sincere but they are also grotesquely misguided.

How, then, could you be sure of God's friendship and reality? I'd suggest that there would be only one way. Suppose God were to stay invisible (because there's no point in blowing your mind with a bizarre experience). But suppose he were to become real to you as any other friend does—communicating with you, allowing you to talk to him, sharing your life experiences and helping to shape your life for you. Answering your prayers. Putting a new power inside you to help you overcome evil with good. Giving you a new quality of love for other people, and especially other Christians, with whom you suddenly discover a shared understanding of experience. And suppose God were to do this, not in a blinding flash, but steadily over a period of weeks, months and years, so that you gradually grew in confidence into a natural reliance upon his faithfulness and dependability. Wouldn't that convince you?

It convinced me. And it has convinced millions of others, down through history. As you will see on p. 106, it is continuing to convince people right around the world day by day. Not just an abstract argument, not just a fluttery feeling inside—but a God who is constantly there and active in the daily affairs of your life. It's exactly what Jesus promised:

> If anyone loves me, he will obey my teaching. My Father will love him, and we will come to him and make our home with him.[6]

Prove it!

Do you find this a convincing answer?
☐ YES ☐ NO ☐ POSSIBLY

!

If you have further objections to the idea of BEING A CHRISTIAN, read some other parts of this section

(pp. 166–186)

?

Alternatively you might be asking:

Can you be sure you know God, or is it all wishful thinking?   (Turn to p. 96)
But is it logical to believe in heaven and hell? People have died and returned to life, but haven't seen them.
(Turn to p. 136)

Christians all look alike—and I couldn't be like that

It's true that people who spend a lot of time together start thinking, dressing and looking alike. And it isn't surprising that you have come across a group of Christians who have a very strong common identity. It happens, and it can't be denied.

But don't fall into the trap of thinking that all Christians are identikit clones of one another. I could introduce you to some extremely original characters! And don't imagine either that God *wants* all Christians to look like one another. After all, if God really created us all, he must have a certain interest in variety—judging by the variations between us! He is not likely to want you to be a copy of someone else. Your inner nature, your personality, your drives and abilities, even your shocking taste in clothes, are things which he has planned into your make-up. Do you think he would really want you to deny your basic nature, when he constructed it with so much care?

And so people who become Christians often find that the experience is really like becoming themselves for the first time in their lives. One of my best friends summed up his conversion experience by saying, 'I feel I don't have to prove anything to anybody any more.' No need to wear a mask, put on a false front, try to impress, jockey for position—just complete freedom to be what you were always meant to be, all along.

Don't look at existing Christians and think, 'I could never be like that.' God doesn't want you like that. God wants you as you are, with everything that he has put into your life still intact, but handed over to his direction and guidance, so that he can bring your life the fulfilment he's been waiting to provide since the moment you were born.

Wouldn't it be silly to miss out on that because you didn't fancy someone else's hairstyle?

⚖️ *Do you find this a convincing answer?*
   ☐ YES   ☐ NO   ☐ POSSIBLY

❗ *If you have further objections to the idea of BEING A CHRISTIAN, read some other parts of this section*
(pp. 166–186)

❓ *Alternatively you might be asking:*

But does conversion really change people at a deep level? (Turn to p. 108)
Hasn't the church always been unfair to women?
(Turn to p. 85)

I can get it all straightened out before I die

Sure you can. Always provided, of course, that you know exactly when that will be. Just when precisely are you planning to leave us?

Quite apart from that little problem, there are other good reasons for not waiting too long before you sort out your relationship with God and find his forgiveness. One is that you may not even reach your death date—even if you knew it! The Bible claims that one of these days human history is going to be wrapped up, and that then there will be no more time to decide.

This is what Jesus was illustrating when he told the story of the five girls who were shut out of the wedding feast because they had fallen asleep, and weren't ready to meet the bridal party when it arrived. People will be left behind, Jesus was saying. It will all come as a tremendous shock to many people who felt they still had years and years in which to make up their minds. But the Bible makes it clear that the time to respond is now. No guarantees are given that the offer will still be open next Tuesday.

Furthermore, if you are eventually going to face up to Jesus Christ and make up your mind about him, is it sensible to delay the process? If Jesus really offers a new quality of life and a security in this troubled world which you'll never get from anywhere else, what's the sense in continuing stubbornly to battle through life without him? All you need is there for the taking. Is there any good reason why you should wait?

Again, the Bible talks about rewards for faithful service once Christians reach the presence of Jesus. If you intend to be there some day and meet his appraisal, wouldn't it be more sensible to stand before him with a whole lifetime of faithfulness behind you, rather than just a hasty beat-the-clock commitment cobbled together in the last five minutes on your deathbed? What is the proper response to someone who died for you, anyway—to give all you have in his service, with deep gratitude and wonder; or to delay taking advantage of his tremendous sacrifice until the last possible moment, when you can't do anything useful for him any longer?

Think again!

Do you find this a convincing answer?
☐ YES   ☐ NO   ☐ POSSIBLY

If you have further objections to the idea of BEING A CHRISTIAN, read some other parts of this section
(pp. 166–186)

Alternatively you might be asking:

What happens after death, anyway? (Turn to p. 118)
Is it possible that I'm just not the religious sort?
(Turn to p. 99)

I'm not good enough for God to accept me

This is perfectly true. In fact, none of us is good enough for God to accept. The *Letter to the Romans* makes this painfully clear: 'There is no-one righteous, not even one; there is no-one who understands, no-one who seeks God.' The whole human race has gone on the run from God. We've tried to exclude him from having any say in the way we live our lives and the decisions we take. Because of our rebellion, none of us is good enough for God.

This means that we are all heading for God's punishment. For if God is a fair, just law-maker—and he is—he must apply the proper penalty when his laws are broken. And that's what the Bible means when it talks about 'hell' (more about this on p. 127). All of the human race stands under God's condemnation.

There is only one way for us to escape that condemnation, and become right with God again. And it's not through anything we can do for ourselves. Our only hope is that someone else would take our place and suffer our punishment for us.

And that—says the Bible—is exactly what Jesus Christ did when he died on the cross. He stood in our place and bore our blame:

> You see, at just the right time, while we were still powerless, Christ died for the ungodly . . . God demonstrates his own love for us in this: while we were still sinners, Christ died for us.[7]

Notice that he didn't die only for those who were of a superior

moral standard to the others. Christ died for the ungodly—full
stop. So no matter how evil or unworthy you may feel, Jesus
Christ is still willing to accept you and forgive you—just as
you are. You don't need to go through some kind of qualifying
round first. You have no need to be cleaned up to make you
ready to accept him. You can come just as you are—like the
dying thief on the cross, who got there with almost his last
breath. If you're willing enough, you're good enough.

So what will you do?

Do you find this a convincing answer?
☐ YES   ☐ NO   ☐ POSSIBLY

*If you have further objections to the idea of BEING A
CHRISTIAN, read some other parts of this section (pp. 166–
186)*

*If you have read this whole section, you're probably ready to
read Section 9. If not, you may wish to go back to the START
HERE page (p. 1) and choose another direction.*

Alternatively you might be asking:

Isn't it ridiculous that God should demand his son's
death before his bloodlust is avenged?

(Turn to p. 19)

Can you be sure you know God, or is it all just wishful
thinking?   (Turn to p. 96)

1. Romans 3:10–12.
2. Jeremiah 13:23; Romans 7:18–19.
3. 2 Corinthians 5:17.
4. Interviewed by *Cosmopolitan* magazine.
5. Luke 16:31.
6. John 14:23.
7. Romans 5:6–8.

YOURSELF

Check out your own position, now that you've surveyed the evidence. How do you feel about the eight areas we've surveyed?

There is	GOD **a strong possibility** **a slight chance** **no chance**	that the God of the Bible exists
Jesus	JESUS **probably was** **possibly was** **certainly wasn't**	all the Gospels claim him to have been
The Bible seems to be	THE BIBLE **substantially reliable** **perhaps reliable** **totally untrustworthy**	
The Church is	THE CHURCH **more impressive than** **just as bad as** **much worse than**	I thought
It looks as if people	CONVERSION **do have** **may have** **don't have**	their lives supernaturally changed
Christianity has a	LIFE AND DEATH **plausible** **possible** **unlikely**	sets of claims about life and death
It is	WORLD PROBLEMS AND TRAGEDIES **possible** **unlikely** **impossible**	that a God of love is at work in the world

	⎱	BEING A CHRISTIAN	⎰	
Living as a	⎰	**the only way**	⎱	to live
Christian is	⎱	**a reasonable way**	⎰	
	⎰	**an outdated, illogical way**	⎱	

Looking at your answers should help you to choose one of the following conclusions:

As a result of reading this book
1. I am satisfied with my original answer
2. I need to change my stance towards Christianity
3. I can see why Christians believe what they do but I am not willing to change my position

---

If your answer was (1)
Please turn to p. 188 for our final message to you.

If your answer was (2)
You may be thinking
   * I need to investigate this further— *if so, turn to p. 190*
   * I want to know how I can become a Christian—
                                         if so, turn to p. 192

If your answer was (3)
You may be:
   * slightly daunted by the implications of being a Christian— *if so, turn to p. 195*
   * still not persuaded by anything you've read—
                                         if so, turn to p. 197
   * unconcerned about the importance of the whole issue—
                                         if so, turn to p. 199

You have come to the conclusion,

> # 'I am satisfied with my original opinions'

That's fine. How do you feel about it? Triumphant? Or disappointed? Or just bored by this book, and more than ready to move on to something else?

If you feel triumphant—'I've read right through a Christian book packed with clever arguments, and they still haven't got me!'—maybe you should ask yourself whether you've approached this book in quite the right spirit. Were you as open-minded about it as you know you should have been? Or were you just looking for flaws in the argument?

If you feel disappointed, because deep down you were willing to be convinced—and you haven't been—then do have patience with us. No one book can answer the questions for everybody. Perhaps you should look at other books on the evidence for Christianity, and see whether or not they can do more for you than we were able to. We suggest some titles below.

If you feel bored by the whole thing, perhaps you haven't grasped the vital importance of the subject we're dealing with here. This isn't just a matter of philosophical speculations or abstruse opinions. It's about a revolutionary relationship with a living God—or not. About a mission to transform this planet—or not. About purpose, meaning and hope in life—or not. About free forgiveness and eternal life, continuing way beyond death—or not.

You will never decide about a more serious issue. If Christianity is true, it is the most startling reality in the universe. If it is false, it is the biggest and cruellest hoax ever foisted on humanity. Either way, you need to engage your mind with the issues and work out what you really think.

So however you feel—triumphant, disappointed or bored—we think you should go on investigating. Don't give up looking until you are absolutely convinced in your own mind that you have examined all the options, fully and comprehensively, and you have decisively rejected Christianity on the basis of the strongest evidence available to you. Perhaps some other books would help you continue searching. Here are some titles which have proved helpful to thousands of people:

Michael Green, *You Must be Joking* (Hodder)
Steve Gaukroger, *It Makes Sense* (SU)
Michael Green, *Ten Myths About Christianity* (Lion)

You have come to the conclusion,

'I need to investigate this further'

Good! If nothing else, this book seems to have convinced you
that there's at least a chance of Jesus' claims being true. It is
good that you are not prepared to jump to conclusions, but
want to look honestly and carefully at the facts. Just remember
what we warned you, right back at the START HERE page:
when you have sorted through the issues in your mind, you
might just find you have to make an important personal
decision. Jesus' claims are not simply a fascinating field for
speculation, a matter of opinion. If you really come to the
conclusion that he was speaking the truth, you can't just say,
'Hmmm! Interesting', and walk away. You will have to do
something about it.

It's like discovering you have won the football pools. You
don't just file the information away in the back of your mind,
thinking, 'I must remember to tell the wife. She'll be quite
interested to know about it.' No—something so big and
revolutionary alters your whole life at the moment it gets to
you.

Having said that, where do you look next? You'll find some
helpful books listed at the top of this page. Or if you've found
this book a little undemanding, intellectually, and you want
something which stretches you more, try Colin Chapman's
The Case for Christianity (Lion), C. S. Lewis's *Mere Christianity*
(Fount), or James Sire's *Why Should Anyone Believe Anything At
All?* (IVP). If you've had enough of reading abstract ideas, get
to know some Christians—real Christians, who believe the
message of the Bible and are honestly submitted to Jesus'
authority—and watch them for a while. See if they ring true.
See if there isn't something extra about their lives which can't
be explained away as just good nature, or an easy-going
personality.

I'm in two minds whether to advise you to go to church. The
reason is that sometimes (especially when a lively church is
holding a guest service directed at outsiders) a church service
can be a tremendous way of finding out about Christianity in

depth; but sometimes church services can seem remote, alien and even boring to outsiders. Result: they sometimes conclude, 'Christianity is just not me.' And that would be a tragic way to walk away from the one thing that can fulfil your life absolutely.

Then there's the Bible. I became a Christian when I looked at the Bible and realized that all the things Christians had told me weren't just their own private ideas—they were really there, in the Bible itself. Since the Bible is (it claims) God's own communication to us, it is the most important book you can go to in order to sort the whole business out. It has a power and conviction all of its own. Don't ever believe it's a totally inscrutable book, which you have no hope of making sense of—a book of riddles and dark sayings which you can only puzzle over. You will understand most of what you read if you follow two simple rules.

(1) Read it in an understandable, modern version—there are lots of good ones to choose from, such as the *Good News Bible* and the *New International Version*.

(2) Start with something that's easy to grasp and get into—such as the *Gospel of Mark*, or the *Gospel of Luke*. Leave *Leviticus* and *Revelation* for later!

But there's one last question we'd like to ask you. If you are honestly undecided about Christianity—fine, investigate further. But are you sure you are hesitating for the right reasons? David Day, who lectures at Durham University, once wrote this:

> 'Being ready' is an odd idea. 'Are you ready for the first night?' someone asks the drama producer. 'Will you be ready for the opening ceremony?' the mayor says to the borough architect. 'Are you ready for the exam?' one student asks another. And nearly always the honest answer is something like: 'Well, I could do with another fortnight . . .'
>
> It is sometimes the case with Christian commitment. It is perilously easy to say to oneself, 'Well, I could do with another fortnight . . .' . . . It is possible that the difficulties you continue to feel are really excuses.[1]

How do you decide whether you have the right reasons for hesitating or not? Day suggests that we should ask ourselves,

'If I got a satisfactory answer to that particular problem, would I then commit my life to Christ? Or would I continue an elaborate game of "Yes, but . . ." in order to keep him at bay?'

Answer the question for yourself. If you are sure that you're not just making excuses and holding off a real moment of decision—carry on as suggested above. But if you feel that the consistent, honest thing to do would be to give Jesus Christ a chance with your life, with no further delay—keep on reading this page.

Either way, we pray that you will get there in the end. For nothing else is more worthwhile. And be encouraged; you have his solemn promise—'If you seek me with all your heart, you will find me!'

You have come to the conclusion,

'I want to know how I can become a Christian'

People have encountered Jesus Christ for the first time in a million different ways. For C. S. Lewis it was on the top deck of a bus going up Headington Hill; for David Sheppard, the cricketer, it was in quiet conversation with a Christian friend; for my own father it was in the middle of a secondary school assembly, while a Bible passage was being read out by a headmaster who didn't believe what he was reading. I can't reduce the process to a standard formula for you. But I can tell you one good way of doing it.

Before I do, let me try to put you off! Jesus Christ never promised an easy time to those who followed him. He advised them to count the cost first. He said, 'Whoever puts his hand to the plough, then turns back, simply cannot be my disciple.' No way do we want to coax you into the kingdom with false promises of thrills, delights and winning the pools within a fortnight. Being a follower of Jesus has its tough side:

The reason the world does not understand us is because it did not understand him . . . Do not be surprised, my brothers, if the world hates you.

How hard it is for the rich to enter the kingdom of God! Indeed, it is easier for a camel to go through the eye of a needle than for a rich man to enter the kingdom of God.

Anyone who does not take his cross and follow me is not worthy of me. Whoever finds his life will lose it, and whoever loses his life for my sake will find it.[2]

What will it cost? Sometimes, the respect and friendship of people who just will not try to understand what has happened to you—who ridicule you, sneer at you and treat you like a simpleton. Sometimes, having to give up habits which are deeply ingrained and a comfortable part of your lifestyle—but are wrong. Following Jesus in a world of starvation, social inequality and political injustice may have implications for your bank balance and some of your free time. You will have to be prepared to associate yourself with a group of Jesus' followers, and start to learn from them, in a good, lively church. You will have to put your own inclinations and convenience second, and do whatever your new Master tells you to do, no matter how reluctant you feel about it.

Some things will have to go, then: your selfishness and independence, your isolation from others, your freewheeling lack of commitment. But they never did you much good anyway. And some things don't have to go: your ability to think rationally and honestly; your sheer enjoyment of life; your sense of purpose and challenge in living. Christian faith will deepen all of those things tremendously!

Undeterred as yet? Good. Let's talk about what exactly you need to do.

Becoming a Christian is not something that happens as a result of an intensive course of churchgoing, or 'instruction in the faith'. It is not a mystical experience that descends in great clouds of emotion when somebody lays hands on you or baptizes you. In fact, you may feel no different. Do you remember how the Christmas carol 'O little town of Bethlehem' puts it? Talking about how quiet and unobserved the birth of Jesus was, it says:

How silently, how silently
    The wondrous gift is given!
So God imparts to human hearts
    The blessings of his heaven;

No ear may hear his coming,
   But in this world of sin,
Where meek souls will receive him, still
   The dear Christ enters in.

Jesus compared the coming of the Holy Spirit into a person's life (which is what happens when you become a Christian) to the invisible wind. 'You hear its sound, but you cannot tell where it comes from or where it is going. So it is with everyone born of the Spirit.'

So what do you do?

Simply talk to God. (In any words you like—no need to learn a special formula.) Tell him that you realize your life falls far short of what he originally intended. That you have been living independent of his guidance and promptings, and that you cannot make a success of life—morally, or in terms of contentment—on your own. That you now realize you need him to rule and govern your experience of living; and that you have heard that Jesus gave his life to gain forgiveness for your shortcomings and wrongdoing. That you now commit your life into his control, as Lord and King from this moment on.

Then find a Christian friend who can help you and advise you about where to go from here. You want to get the very best out of living the Christian life, and not just have a five-minute thrill which fades away quickly. So your new brothers and sisters can be very important, especially right at the outset, in making sure that all is going well. There are good books you can read, too; we recommend Michael Green's *New Life New Lifestyle* (Hodder) and *The Fight* by John White (IVP).

If you have just done what we have suggested—congratulations! And welcome to the family of God. We know that you have just begun on the most exciting journey of your life. You are going to find out things about yourself, about the faithfulness of God, and about your potential with him in charge, which you'd never dream possible at this moment.

But many readers will have skimmed through this section simply out of curiosity. (And quite right too: I wouldn't want to spend this much on buying a book, and then not read every page!) Perhaps you have no personal intention of doing anything about it. Or you did, but our description makes i all seem too simple. You're daunted now, in case it doesn't work . . .

Listen. Millions of people down through history have found that Jesus Christ always keeps his promises. Around the world right now, over 420,000,000 people claim to have each had a personal, individual, life-transforming experience of the friendship and reality of Jesus. It could be a delusion. But what a massive delusion it would be!

Can you afford to miss something as big as this? Have you a better answer to the mysteries of life, the human craving for fulfilment and certainty, your own moral shortcomings and your need of forgiveness? Have you any answer?

We challenge you to take God at his word.

You have come to the conclusion,

> # 'I am slightly daunted by the implications of becoming a Christian'

Therefore you are unwilling to change your position.

You have a rare and refreshing honesty. That's great. But just before you leave this book, perhaps you should ask yourself three questions.

First, are you sure you have understood clearly what you would be rejecting? Being a Christian is not a spare-time hobby like train spotting and building canoes. When a man joins himself to Jesus Christ, it means slightly more than joining a a fan club or a political party. So be clear about what you're turning down.

If Christians are right, you would be rejecting a home in heaven. Full and free forgiveness for all your wrongdoing. The chance of a new life beginning inside you, slowly turning you into the You you've always wanted to be but could never make yourself—rebuilding your life the way God intended, giving you a new self-respect and humility, the joy of a mind at peace with itself.

You would be turning your back on a loving Father who has

been watching you ever since your birth, waiting for the moment when you would recognize his reality and turn to accept the love he longs to pour upon you. You would be rejecting the most costly, awful, painful sacrifice anybody ever made for anyone else—when you look at the cross of Jesus and say, 'No thanks.'

You would be walking away from your only chance of making sense of the problems and complexities, the unsolved agonizing questions, of this life. And much more besides. Have you really calculated the cost of saying No?

Second question. Is your reason for refusal good enough? You are not saying No because you are intellectually convinced that it is all a load of rubbish. You are not saying No because you have found a better, more adequate philosophy. You're turning away simply because you can't handle anything so big and demanding. Is that really how much you think of yourself?

You are right to see commitment as a big and demanding thing. But you are wrong to think you couldn't make it. Once a person becomes a Christian, all the resources of God start to become real—his peace, his assurance, his ability to resist evil. It's not a matter of struggling forlornly on your own to maintain a Christian stance. It's more like coming home. Walking into a new world where—you suddenly realize—you should have been years before. Finding a new source of stability and a new emotional centre in the reality of a God who shows his love for you in a million ways, and will never let you down or let you go.

So we're not saying, 'Trust yourself! You can make it if you try.' We're saying instead, 'No, quite right, you'd never make it on your own. But you won't be on your own. Trust Jesus, not yourself, and he will give you everything you need.'

And now the final question. *What will happen if you do walk away?* For Christianity is not an optional extra which you can add on to your lifestyle if you feel so disposed. ('Try Jesus, the great new wonder drug—that's if you're not doing anything this evening, of course.') If Jesus is the only Son of God, and gave his life in a cataclysmic once-for-all event to open up a chance of forgiveness for human beings, then what he offers is unique, vital and indispensable. If you reject it the bottom will drop out of your future.

Let me predict three things that will happen if you dismiss Jesus Christ. First, the rest of your life will be an anticlimax. Oh, there will be moments of joy, triumph, achievement. But deep down at the back of it all you'll know you haven't found the big answers yet. And you'll have the nagging memory that once a chance of finding them opened itself up in front of you. And you walked away.

Second, you will gradually lose the ability to respond to Jesus Christ. In my experience, when people have come close to commitment and walked away, it gets harder and harder for them to do anything about it thereafter. 'Now is the accepted time,' urges the Bible. 'Seek the Lord while he may be found! Call on him while he is near!'[3]

Third, you still have the judgement of God to face one day. How tragic to approach this unprotected and unforgiven— when Jesus Christ has done absolutely everything necessary to wipe your record clean in an instant. I don't propose to dwell on the consequences the Bible spells out for those who face the wrath of God. But it would be foolish not to take them seriously.

Think about it. Hard. And if you decide you need to change your mind, turn to p. 192 and take it from there. We hope you will.

You have come to the conclusion,

'I am still not persuaded by anything I've read'

Therefore you are unwilling to change your position.

There could be several reasons for coming to this conclusion. I wonder if yours is one of the following list?

You might feel the whole book is too glib and superficial. That we are skating over serious problems very quickly. Admittedly, we've tried to cram a lot into just a few pages, and that can sometimes give the impression that we're laying down the law and relying on unfairly selective evidence.

But don't assume that there are no deeper arguments, or that we've stated all the evidence there is! If you need a book which will take you more deeply into the evidence in one area or another, there are plenty to choose from. For example, if you wanted to study the evidence for the resurrection in more detail, you could look at John Wenham's *Easter Enigma* (Paternoster), Frank Morison's *Who Moved the Stone?* (OM), or Michael Green's *Man Alive!* (IVP). If the relationship of science and Christianity is giving you problems, try Donald Mackay's *The Clockwork Image* (IVP) or his *Human Science and Human Dignity* (Hodder). Browse round any good Christian bookshop and you'll find lots to interest you.

Or you might be saying, 'Sorry, not persuaded', because you came to the book with your mind already made up. Have you really looked at the arguments we've used with objectivity and an honestly open mind?

Or it might be that you would like to be persuaded—you're quite ready to believe what we say, if only we can convince you—but nothing in this book has built up enough conviction in your mind to clinch the deal. You're still waiting for the one missing piece of the jigsaw, the one conclusive bit of evidence, which will prove beyond a shadow of a doubt that Jesus' claims were true. I have bad news for you. You're not going to get it.

You can't prove the reality of Christianity by arguments alone. You can built up a very good case; but you'll just end up with a pile of evidence on one side saying, 'Yes, it's true', and a pile of evidence on the other side saying, 'No, it's rubbish', and some days one pile will look larger than the other. But you'll never be able to make up your mind conclusively, because the next day the other pile may seem a little bigger . . . The only way of being certain, beyond any shadow of a doubt, is to take the risk of inviting Jesus Christ to become Lord and king of your life, and proving in your own experience that he is real. I can't prove him to you with clever arguments. Only you can prove him to yourself.

Are you ready to do that? Or do you feel you still need to sort out the facts a little bit more? Either way, we have some advice for you. To find out how to invite Jesus Christ into your life, turn to p. 192. To find out how to explore the evidence a bit more, look at p. 190.

You have come to the conclusion,

> # 'I am unconcerned about the importance of the whole issue'

And therefore you are unwilling to change your position.

You're joking! Aren't you? If there really is a creator in charge of this universe, who doesn't see you simply as Humanoid No. XY403/ 256A8, but as someone whom he loves and cares for in a unique way . . . And if he is offering to transform your life by adding a dimension of meaning, purpose and sheer joy that you'll never find anywhere else . . . And if the result of neglecting his offer is to face judgement and eternity alone . . . What issue could be more important?

I wonder why you *don't* see it as important. Perhaps it's because you're thinking, 'You can never know the truth of these things anyway. When all's said and done, you just have to believe. It's all really a matter of opinion.' But Christianity isn't about things that can't be proved. It's about being able to verify, here and now in your daily experience, that God is real and alive. Read through the New Testament. See how often Christian writers use the word 'know'—not 'hope' or 'feel'!—with utter, calm confidence:

> I know whom I have believed, and am convinced that he is able to guard what I have entrusted to him . . .

> We know that we are children of God . . . We know also that the Son of God has come and has given us understanding, so that we may know him who is true.

> If you hold to my teaching . . . you will know the truth, and the truth will set you free.[4]

If this is true—that you can know for sure!—it is fantastic. If it is false, it is dangerous stupidity. Either way—it's important!

Or you may be thinking, 'I may not be religious, but I'm as good as anyone else. God will probably accept me anyway, assuming he exists.' If this is your idea, you must have skipped pp. 127–129—go back and have a look at it. The fact is,

God doesn't accept people on the basis of their perfect moral performance. He wants, not performance, but surrender. You can live a very impressive life, but if it's all lived in rebellion against him, keeping him obstinately out on the sidelines, why should he feel pleased with you?

I have a daughter who is sometimes naughty. When she misbehaves, our relationship is strained—and I hate it. I long for her to say she's sorry and make friends again. It would not make me happy at all if she continued to live in our house with a barrier of hostility between her and me. She might be living a life of stupendous ethical quality on her side of the barrier, but I would get no joy out of that. What I would be longing for would be the chance to make friends again.

And God looks at us like that.

But perhaps you're thinking, 'This issue is unimportant because I want to live just one day at a time. I have enough problems here and now, without worrying about an afterlife, heaven and hell. I'll deal with God, if there is a God, when I finally meet him face to face.'

However, the Bible insists, 'Now is the accepted time, now is the time of rescue.' It makes no promises about tomorrow. In fact, in several of the stories Jesus told, we are clearly warned that some people will leave it just too late. The time to sort it out is today.

You couldn't 'live just one day at a time' in any other area of life. Suppose you were driving along a mountain road when a policeman flagged you down and warned that you were heading for a sheer drop. Would you really answer, 'I'll handle that problem when I come to it, thank you', and drive on? I doubt it.

Or suppose you were told that Queen Elizabeth would be dropping in on you for tea the following afternoon. Would you simply mutter, 'I'll deal with that problem when I see her', and carry on as usual? Or would you run round in circles making preparations?

There are some future events you have to think about today. That's why we have insurance policies and pension schemes. That's why you book your holidays early, if you're wise, and do your Christmas shopping before Christmas Eve. And that's why you ought to consider leaving this book with a slightly different verdict!

(If this makes sense to you, and you do want to reconsider, turn back to p. 188 and select a different option.)

1. David Day, *op. cit.*, 106–7.
2. 1 John 3:l, 13; Luke 18:25; Matthew 10:38–9.
3. 2 Corinthians 6:2; Isaiah 55:6.4. 2 Timothy 1:12; I John 5:–19–20; John 6:32.

A quick guide to the page you need

If you're trying to find our answer to one specific question
—and you don't want to plough through the whole book
looking for it—here's what to do.

1. Decide which of these categories it falls into:

   questions about GOD (complete list on p. 5);
   JESUS (p. 22);
   THE BIBLE (p. 45);
   THE CHURCH (p. 68);
   CONVERSION (p. 91);
   LIFE AND DEATH (p. 115);
   WORLD PROBLEMS AND TRAGEDIES (p. 142);
   BEING A CHRISTIAN (p. 166).

2. Look it up in the complete list, given on the page indicated
   above.

3. If it isn't there, ask yourself:
   —Could this question be listed under another category?
   —If it isn't listed at all, are there some *underlying assumptions* in it which this book does answer? (Read the top of
   page 3 if you need more guidance on this).

Good hunting! We're sure you'll find most things you're
looking for in there somewhere! Because—as we said at the
beginning—there aren't really a great number of objections
commonly raised against Christian claims. The wonder is that
so many people trot out the same stale, tired arguments time
and again!